COOKING WITH
Bon Appétit

COOKING WITH
Bon Appétit

Breads

THE KNAPP PRESS
Publishers
Los Angeles

Copyright © 1985 by Knapp Communications Corporation

Published by The Knapp Press
5900 Wilshire Boulevard, Los Angeles, California 90036

Library of Congress Cataloging in Publication Data

Breads.

  (Cooking with Bon appétit)
  Includes index.
  1. Bread. I. Series.
TX769.B7757 1985   641.8'15   85-9860
ISBN 0-89535-168-4

On the cover: *An assortment of rolls, loaves and baguettes*

Printed and bound in the United States of America

10   9   8   7   6   5   4

❦ Contents

❦ Foreword

More and more people are baking their own bread and finding it uniquely satisfying. Part of the satisfaction is in bypassing mediocre commercial loaves, but there is much more to it than that: It is exhilarating to see a kneaded yeast dough become, as if by sleight of hand, silky, smooth and resilient; to watch it rise to double or triple its original volume; to enjoy the wonderful aroma as it bakes.

Quick breads, too, have a homey appeal all their own. Even though they take only minutes to prepare, freshly baked muffins or biscuits give a meal a whole new personality. An assortment of quick breads is a great addition to a breakfast or brunch buffet, and a decoratively wrapped fruit or nut loaf is a perfect gift at any time of year.

This book celebrates bread in all its international varieties. It offers basic white and whole-grain loaves and rolls, festive and fancifully shaped holiday specialties and a large selection of quick breads—including muffins, crackers, biscuits and flatbreads. There is something for every occasion—as well as for the times when you just have a hankering to dig in and knead a batch of dough for the sheer fun of it.

Discover the pleasures of baking bread at home. We may not live by bread alone, but with a selection like this you just might be tempted to!

1 ❦ Basic White and Whole Wheat Breads

This first chapter offers basic white and whole wheat loaves in a wide assortment of styles and textures. It begins with two simple French bread recipes, one especially adapted for the processor. From here the variations could go on forever: There are breads with potato, cheese, cornmeal, oats, molasses and other additions, as well as a range of whole wheat breads from light and delicate to dark and chewy. You will even find an English muffin loaf developed expressly for the microwave oven.

Also included in this section is information about two essential ingredients—yeast and flour. Read through this boxed text (pages 4 to 5 and 8 to 9) before you begin, especially if you feel the least bit intimidated about breadmaking. You will see that, far from demanding great exactitude, bread recipes are flexible and forgiving. You can speed them up or slow them down to suit your convenience; the rising process can be interrupted for hours or even days, if need be, by chilling the dough; and there is tremendous leeway for experimenting with a multitude of different flours and flavorings.

After a few introductory sessions you will see how easy it really is to make your own bread, and it won't be much longer before you have the confidence of a master baker.

French Bread

To give the loaves a crusty exterior, soak a brick in water overnight, then drain it and put it into the oven with the bread to create steam. Best served the same day as baked.

Makes 12 small loaves

1 envelope dry yeast
3 cups warm water (105° to 115°F)
8 cups (about) unbleached all purpose flour
1 tablespoon salt

Cornmeal

1 egg white beaten with
1 tablespoon water (glaze)

Soak brick in water overnight.

Sprinkle yeast onto ¼ cup warm water in bowl of electric mixer fitted with dough hook; stir to dissolve. Let stand 5 minutes. Add remaining flour ½ cup at a time until slightly sticky dough forms. Mix until smooth and elastic, about 8 minutes. Turn dough out onto lightly floured surface and knead until smooth and no longer sticky, adding more flour if necessary, about 3 minutes. (Dough can also be mixed and kneaded by hand.) Grease large bowl and add dough, turning to coat surface. Cover with damp towel. Let rise at room temperature 8 hours. Punch dough down and knead on lightly floured surface until smooth, about 2 minutes. Return to greased bowl, turning to coat entire surface. Cover with damp towel and let rise in warm draft-free area until doubled in volume, about 2 hours.

Grease baking sheets and sprinkle with cornmeal. Punch dough down and knead on lightly floured surface until smooth, about 2 minutes. Divide into 12 pieces. Pat each into 4 × 7-inch rectangle. Roll up jelly roll fashion, starting at one long side. Pinch seams to seal. Arrange seam side down on prepared sheets, spacing 3 inches apart. Let rise until almost doubled in volume, about 45 minutes.

Preheat oven to 475°F. Remove brick from water and place in oven. Make 3 diagonal slashes in loaves. Brush with egg glaze. Bake 10 minutes. Reduce oven to 350°F and continue baking until loaves sound hollow when tapped on bottom, about 35 minutes. Cool on racks before serving.

Processor French Bread

This recipe can be mixed in any standard-size food processor.

Makes one 1½-pound loaf

Glaze
1 egg
½ teaspoon salt

Dough
1 envelope dry yeast
1 teaspoon sugar
1 cup plus 2 tablespoons warm water (105°F to 115°F)

2 cups bread flour
1 cup unbleached all purpose flour
1 teaspoon salt

Cornmeal

For glaze: Insert steel knife into processor and mix egg with salt until blended, about 2 seconds. Transfer to small dish, cover and refrigerate. Do not clean processor work bowl.

For dough: Oil large bowl; set aside. Combine yeast, sugar and water in small mixing bowl and let stand until foamy, about 10 minutes.

Combine flours and salt in processor work bowl. With machine running, add yeast through feed tube and mix until dough is moist and elastic, about 40 seconds. If dough seems too moist, add more flour 1 tablespoon at a time and mix until consistency is correct. Transfer dough to oiled bowl, turning to coat all surfaces. Cover bowl with damp towel and let stand in warm draft-free area until doubled, about 1 hour (an oven preheated to lowest setting for 2 minutes and then turned off works well; cushion bottom of bowl with pot holder). Punch dough down, cover with plastic wrap and refrigerate a minimum of 8 hours or up to 5 days.

About 3 hours before serving, grease or oil French bread pan or baking sheet and sprinkle with cornmeal. Roll dough out on lightly floured board into 12-inch rectangle. Roll up lengthwise (as for jelly roll), pinching ends and seam tightly. Place dough seam side down in pan or on baking sheet and stretch gently to fit (it should measure 12 inches). Cover with damp towel and let stand in warm draft-free area until doubled, about 1½ hours.

About 15 minutes before baking, position rack in center of oven and cover with unglazed quarry tiles (if available). Preheat oven to 425°F. Slash top of loaf and brush with glaze, being careful not to drip glaze onto pan. Bake until loaf is deeply colored and sounds hollow when tapped on bottom, about 25 to 30 minutes. Remove and let cool on wire rack.

Sheepherder's Bread

Traditionally, the herder baked this bread in a cast-iron Dutch oven in an earthen pit with sagebrush embers surrounding the pot. Before slicing the loaf, he would slash a cross on top. He fed the first slice to his sheepdog.

Makes 1 large loaf

3 cups hot water (from tap)	2 teaspoons salt
⅔ cup butter, room temperature	2 envelopes dry yeast
½ cup sugar	9 cups all purpose flour

Generously grease large bowl and 6-quart cast-iron Dutch oven with tight-fitting lid; grease lid. Combine water, butter, sugar and salt in another large bowl and stir until butter is melted. Let cool to lukewarm, about 110°F. Add yeast and stir until dissolved. Let stand in warm place until bubbly, about 10 to 15 minutes. Add 4 cups flour and beat with wooden spoon (or transfer to heavy-duty mixer) and beat until thick batter forms. Gradually stir in 4½ cups flour until dough is stiff and no longer sticky. Sprinkle work surface with remaining ½ cup flour. Knead dough until smooth and elastic, about 10 minutes. Place in greased bowl, turning to coat entire surface. Cover with towel and let rise in warm draft-free area until doubled in bulk, about 1½ to 2 hours.

Punch dough down. Transfer to prepared Dutch oven. Cover and let rise in warm draft-free area until dough touches lid, about 30 to 35 minutes.

Preheat oven to 375°F. Bake bread, covered, 10 minutes. Remove lid and continue baking until bread is deep brown, about 50 minutes. Turn out onto rack and cool before serving.

English Muffin Bread

This uses the microwave oven to its best advantage.

Makes two 8½ × 4½-inch loaves

Cornmeal	2 envelopes dry yeast
2 cups milk	1 tablespoon sugar
½ cup water	2 teaspoons salt
5 cups all purpose flour	¼ teaspoon baking soda

Grease two 8½ × 4½- inch glass or ceramic loaf pans. Sprinkle with cornmeal, shaking out excess. Combine milk and water in 1-quart measure. Heat in microwave on High until warmed through, about 3 to 4 minutes. (If using probe, set at 125°F.) Mix 3 cups flour, yeast, sugar, salt and baking soda in large bowl. Add warm milk mixture and beat well. Blend in remaining flour and stir until dough is stiff. Divide dough between pans. Cover and let rise in warm draft-free area 45 minutes.

Cook loaves one at a time in microwave on High for 6 to 6½ minutes, turning once. Let stand 5 minutes before removing from pan. Slice loaves thinly and toast before serving.

❦ *About Yeast*

Fresh yeast is sold in ³/₅-ounce cakes that should be creamy-white or light tan in color and firm in texture; if it is brown and crumbly it has lost its potency. It should be kept under refrigeration; it may also be frozen. To use, crumble and stir into lukewarm water. Let this stand for about five minutes before mixing with dry ingredients.

Dry yeast is most commonly available in ¼-ounce envelopes. One envelope is equivalent to a cake of fresh yeast. Many bakers find the dry form more convenient to have on hand because it keeps without refrigeration for up to a year. Each envelope has an expiration date on the label; after this date the yeast will have lost some of its leavening power. Before you use it you must rehydrate it by sprinkling it over lukewarm water. (A pinch of sugar added to this mixture causes yeast to foam and appear more active but it is not critical to the process.) Let it stand for about ten minutes. Before combining with dry ingredients, stir the yeast-water mixture if it is not smooth.

Fast-rising yeast is a recent arrival on the market. Made from an unusually active strain, it is said to cut the rising time of dough in half. It is available in ¼-ounce envelopes and can be substituted for regular dry yeast in recipes. The makers recommend a special mixing method: Combine with the dry ingredients, then add any liquid (except eggs), which must be heated.

How It Works
Making yeast dough is a special experience, one that involves all the senses. After the yeast mixture and dry ingredients are blended, the dough is kneaded. This distributes the yeast evenly and ensures that the resulting loaf will have a uniform texture. Kneading also develops gluten, a protein in the flour, which enables the dough to stretch evenly and hold the bubbles of gas released by the yeast.

After kneading, the dough is covered with plastic wrap or a damp cloth, to prevent its surface from drying out, and placed in a warm draft-free place. At this point, the yeast has everything it needs to grow: warmth and food. The cells become very active as they eat, multiply, and convert sugar and starch to tiny bubbles of carbon dioxide, an odorless and tasteless gas. The gas tries to escape from the mass, creating pressure and causing it to rise.

Recipes usually specify that yeast dough rise until doubled. An easy way to tell whether this process is complete is to press two fingers into it. If the imprints remain, rising is sufficient.

Vioen Bread

Makes two 8¹/₂ × 4¹/₂-inch loaves

2¼ cups water
½ cup peeled grated baking potato
3 tablespoons honey
3 tablespoons butter-flavored solid vegetable shortening, room temperature
4 teaspoons salt
1 envelope dry yeast

5 cups unbleached all purpose flour
1¼ cups coarse-ground undegerminated yellow cornmeal*

Butter-flavored solid vegetable shortening

At this point, the dough is punched down—accomplished by kneading lightly or folding the dough in three and patting it firmly. This brings it back to its orginal size and redistributes the gas bubbles that have formed. It also ensures that the finished product will have a good uniform texture and helps to strengthen the yeast for the second (and final) rising.

The dough may now be shaped into its finished form and left to rise again. If the end product is to be thin and crisp, this rising time is brief, but a loaf of bread will need to double again and some very light cakes need to triple in volume before baking.

During baking the activity of the yeast becomes spectacular. In the heat of the oven it produces a large amount of gas. The gas bubbles continue to expand for the first five or ten minutes of baking and compel the dough to rise rapidly. Eventually the internal temperature of the dough becomes hot enough to kill the yeast and the mixture ceases to grow in size.

Yeast is sensitive to extremes of temperature. Cold retards or checks its growth; excessive heat kills it. Most bread doughs rise best between 70°F and 80°F. Exceptions are those such as brioche, which contain a high proportion of butter: they need slightly cooler rising temperatures so that the butter does not melt and leak out.

Yet within these limits there is great flexibility. In many cases, you may retard rising with no serious consequences. Assemble the yeast dough and let it rise for about 15 minutes, then refrigerate or freeze it. The dough will continue to expand slowly, stopping once it is thoroughly chilled. When ready to bake, bring it to room temperature and let it finish rising.

If dough rises too much it can acquire a sour flavor; in extreme cases of neglect its careful shape can collapse. Underrisen dough yields heavy loaves and cakes. Mastering the process comes with practice, but slight errors in either direction will not necessarily ruin the finished product.

The proportion of yeast to flour affects the amount of rising time. The more yeast, the shorter it will be. The cook in a hurry can increase the amount slightly but too much will give bread a strong, sour taste. Most experts agree that the flavor of bread is best if a small amount of yeast is used and the dough is allowed to rise slowly.

Yeast works more efficiently in a large amount of dough than in a small one because a large mass will always retain its warmth much better.

Bring water and potato to boil in medium saucepan and cook until potato is translucent and tender, about 5 minutes. Cool to 105°F. Stir in honey, 3 tablespoons shortening, salt and yeast. Let stand until foamy and proofed, about 10 minutes.

Preheat oven to lowest setting. Grease large bowl. Sift flour into another large bowl. Mix in cornmeal. Make well in center. Add potato mixture to well. Gradually incorporate flour into liquid. Knead in bowl until smooth and elastic, about 15 minutes. Add dough to greased bowl, turning to coat entire surface. Cover with kitchen towel. Turn oven off. Let dough rise in oven until doubled in volume, about 1 hour.

Return oven to lowest setting. Grease two 8½ × 4½ × 2½-inch pans. Punch dough down. Knead 3 to 4 minutes. Divide in half and transfer to prepared pans. Cover loaves with kitchen towels. Turn oven off. Let dough rise in oven until 1 inch above pans, about 50 minutes.

Remove towels from loaves. Increase oven temperature to 350°F. Bake loaves until golden brown, about 30 minutes. Remove from pans. Rub each loaf with shortening. Cool at least 1 hour before slicing.

*Available at natural foods stores.

Ricotta Cheese Bread

This versatile loaf can be made sweet with the addition of candied fruit or savory with chopped fresh herbs. It is excellent plain or toasted.

Makes one 9 × 5-inch loaf or two 7 × 3 × 2-inch loaves

¼ cup milk, scalded and cooled to 105°F to 115°F
1 tablespoon dry yeast
1 tablespoon sugar for savory loaf or ¼ cup sugar for sweet loaf
6 tablespoons (¾ stick) butter, room temperature
2 eggs, room temperature
2 teaspoons salt
1½ cups ricotta cheese
¼ cup mixed chopped fresh herbs (parsley, chives, marjoram, basil, rosemary, oregano)

or

1 cup mixed glacéed fruit and ¼ cup raisins soaked in 2 tablespoons rum
1 teaspoon vanilla
Generous pinch of freshly grated nutmeg

3 to 4 cups all purpose flour

1 egg yolk blended with 2 tablespoons milk

Stir milk, yeast and sugar in large bowl until yeast dissolves. Let stand 20 minutes. Beat in butter, eggs and salt until smooth. Blend in ricotta and herbs for savory loaf, or ricotta and glacéed fruit, raisins, vanilla and nutmeg for sweet loaf. Beat in 3 cups flour until smooth and slightly elastic, about 5 minutes. If mixture appears too moist, beat in up to 1 cup more flour; and dough should be soft not dry. Transfer to buttered bowl, turning to coat entire surface. Cover dough and let rise in warm draft-free area until doubled in volume, about 1½ hours.

Punch dough down. Let rise again in warm draft-free area until doubled.

Butter 9 × 5-inch loaf pan. Punch dough down. Form into smooth loaf and place in prepared pan. Let rise ⅔ up pan. Brush loaf with egg glaze.

Preheat oven to 375°F. Bake loaf 50 minutes. Let cool in pan 5 minutes, then invert loaf onto rack.

For 2 small loaves, divide dough in half and bake in two 7 × 3 × 2-inch pans. You can also create 1 small loaf of each type at once: Make dough with savory sponge. After adding ricotta, divide dough in half. Add 2 tablespoons chopped fresh herbs to 1 portion. To other portion, add ½ cup glacéed fruit, 2 tablespoons sugar, 2 tablespoons raisins, ½ teaspoon vanilla and pinch of freshly grated nutmeg.

Pane alla Contadina (Peasant Bread)

The starter for this bread must be prepared three days ahead.

Makes 2 loaves

1 yeast cake
1 cup lukewarm water (90°F to 105°F)
1 cup whole wheat flour

4 cups bread flour
1½ cups lukewarm water (90°F to 105°F)

2 teaspoons salt
1 teaspoon sugar

2 cups bread flour
½ teaspoon baking soda

Combine yeast and 1 cup lukewarm water in large bowl, stirring until completely dissolved. Add 1 cup whole wheat flour and mix well. Cover tightly and let stand at room temperature 3 days, stirring down once each day.

One day before baking, add 4 cups bread flour to starter with remaining lukewarm water, salt and sugar, blending well. Cover and let stand at room temperature for 24 hours.

Punch dough down. Add remaining 2 cups bread flour with baking soda. Transfer to heavy-duty mixer fitted with dough hook and knead until dough is smooth and elastic, about 10 minutes (or knead by hand on floured surface for 15 to 20 minutes).

Divide dough in half. Form each portion into round or oblong shape. Place on floured surface, cover with damp towel and let rise in warm draft-free area until doubled, about 1 to 3 hours.

Line oven rack with quarry tiles. Preheat oven to 400°F. Set pan filled with boiling water at one side of rack in oven to provide moisture. Place loaves directly on hot tiles and spray lightly with water. Make ½-inch slash down center of loaves with knife. Bake loaves 5 minutes, then spray generously again with water. Bake until loaves sound hollow when tapped on bottom, about 45 minutes. Remove loaves from oven and let cool on rack.

Whole Wheat Buttermilk Bread

Makes 2 baguettes

Glaze
1 large egg
½ teaspoon salt

Bread
1 envelope dry yeast
1 teaspoon sugar
½ cup plus 2 tablespoons warm water (105°F to 115°F)

2⅓ cups bread flour
⅔ cup whole wheat flour

1¼ teaspoons salt
½ cup plus 1 tablespoon warm buttermilk (105°F to 115°F)
2 tablespoons (¼ stick) unsalted butter, room temperature

Cornmeal

For glaze: Insert steel knife into processor and mix egg with salt 2 seconds; remove and set aside. Do not clean work bowl.

For bread: Oil large mixing bowl and set aside. Combine yeast and sugar with warm water in small bowl and let stand until foamy, about 10 minutes.

Combine 2 cups bread flour with whole wheat flour and salt in processor work bowl. With machine running, pour yeast mixture and buttermilk through feed tube and mix until dough forms ball. Add butter and mix until dough pulls away from sides of bowl and is smooth and elastic, about 40 seconds. If dough is too wet, add remaining ⅓ cup bread flour 1 tablespoon at a time and mix.

🍏 All About Flours

Since bread consists of little but moistened flour, leavening and seasonings, its character depends largely on the type of flour used to make it. *Hard or strong wheat* provides the best flour for yeast-risen loaves because it helps create a high percentage of gluten, the elastic protein that forms a rigid framework for trapping gases released by the yeast. Breads made with high-gluten flours have greater volume and more interesting texture.

Like other wheats and grains, hard wheat can be milled through hot steel rollers or it can be stone-ground the old-fashioned way between two heavy circular stones that coarsely crush the grain. *Whole wheat flour* (also known as *whole grain, whole meal, and graham flour*) for dark breads is ground from the entire wheat kernel, whereas *white bread flour* for lighter loaves is ground only from part of it. Whole wheat flour contains more nutrients than white flour, but has a shorter shelf life. Ground coarse, medium or fine, it is quite dense and should be mixed with at least ⅓ white flour for bread. Flours are also milled from just the wheat germ and bran. Although they are too coarse to be used by themselves, when combined with other flour they contribute a nutty texture to dark breads.

When white hard wheat bread flour is unavailable, *all purpose flour* is an excellent substitute. This lower-gluten blend of hard and soft wheats is usually enriched with iron, thiamin, riboflavin, niacin and other nutrients to replace minerals lost during the milling process. Moreover, all purpose flour is generally bleached, although the silkier texture of unbleached flour is preferred for baking.

In addition to wheat, other grains and plants are ground into flours that add intriguing flavors and textures to bread. Of these *grain flours* rye is the only one capable of developing gluten. The amount is negligible, however, producing a sticky dough rather than an elastic one. For this reason, breads

Transfer to oiled bowl, turning to coat all surfaces. Cover bowl with damp towel. Let stand in warm draft-free area until dough has doubled in volume, about 1 hour (an oven preheated to lowest setting for 2 minutes and then turned off works well; cushion bottom of bowl with pot holder).

Meanwhile, grease double French bread pan or baking sheet and sprinkle lightly with cornmeal. Transfer dough to lightly floured surface and divide in half. Roll 1 piece into rectangle, then roll up lengthwise, pinching ends and seam tightly. Arrange loaf seam side down in half of prepared pan or sheet. Repeat with remaining dough. Cover loaves with damp towel. Let stand in warm draft-free area until doubled, approximately 45 minutes.

Position rack in center of oven and preheat to 425°F. Brush tops of loaves with glaze, being careful not to drip onto pan. Bake until bread is golden brown and sounds hollow when tapped on bottom, 25 to 30 minutes. Remove from pan and let cool on rack.

🍏

based on grain flours require more leavening and a ratio of at least half wheat flour. Along with rye, the most popular bread grains are oatmeal and white or yellow cornmeal, which are favored for their sweetness and soft, crumbly texture. *Prepared tortilla flour,* a cornmeal ground from dried corn kernels that have been soaked in water and unslaked lime, is intended only for tortillas. The moist, richly colored *barley flour* appears in Scandinavian flat-breads. *Soya flour* (from toasted soybeans) is high in fat and protein and is used to enrich dough. A lowfat *soy flour* (from the raw beans) is also available.

Great Hints

- The percentage of moisture in flour varies according to how it was processed and how it is stored. Because of this, the amount of liquid needed for a bread recipe may change from batch to batch. Mix dry ingredients with just enough liquid to make a soft, pliable dough.
- Bread flour absorbs more liquid than all purpose flour and must be beaten longer to expand its gluten potential.
- To prevent breads made with bran flour from being dry, mix bran with liquid called for in recipe and let stand several hours before proceeding.
- For a crunchy, nutty texture, replace about ½ cup of flour with pre-cooked whole wheat berries or cracked wheat.
- The shelf life of white flour is 1 to 2 years. To store it, transfer to tightly closed container to prevent moisture absorption. Keep in cool dark spot.
- Nonwhite flours should be used within 3 to 4 months. To keep high-fat flours such as whole wheat, wheat germ, oatmeal and soy fresh, store in freezer.

Honey Whole Wheat Bread

Makes one 9 × 5-inch loaf

1¾ cups all purpose flour
1¼ cups whole wheat flour
1½ teaspoons salt

1 envelope dry yeast
1¼ cups warm water (105°F to 115°F)

2 tablespoons honey
2 tablespoons (¼ stick) unsalted butter, room temperature

Butter, room temperature

Combine flours and salt and mix well. Generously grease 9 × 5-inch loaf pan.

Sprinkle yeast over water in large bowl of electric mixer and let proof about 5 minutes. Add honey, 2 tablespoons butter and half of flour mixture and beat 2 minutes on medium speed. Add remaining flour and beat until smooth, about 1 minute. Cover and let rise in warm, draft-free area until doubled in volume, about 45 minutes.

Stir batter down with wooden spoon and beat about 25 strokes. Turn into prepared pan. Cover and let rise until 1 inch below top edge of pan, about 45 minutes.

Preheat oven to 375°F. Bake until bread is well browned, 40 to 50 minutes. Brush top with butter. Remove from pan and let cool on rack before slicing.

Stone-Ground Wheat Bread

Stone-ground flour gives this loaf an interesting texture and superb flavor.

Makes one 8 × 4-inch loaf

1¼ cups warm water (105°F to 115°F)
1 envelope dry yeast
2 cups stone-ground wheat flour
1 cup plus 2 tablespoons bread flour
2 tablespoons (¼ stick) unsalted butter, room temperature

2 tablespoons firmly packed brown sugar
2 teaspoons salt

Butter, room temperature

Grease 8 × 4-inch loaf pan. Combine water and yeast in large mixing bowl. Stir in 1 cup wheat flour, ½ cup bread flour, butter, brown sugar and salt. Beat at medium speed of electric mixer 2 minutes. Add remaining flours and beat 1½ minutes longer. Cover with plastic wrap and let rise in warm area until doubled, about 1 hour.

Beat dough about 30 strokes with wooden spoon. Turn into prepared pan. Cover and let rise until doubled, about 45 minutes.

Preheat oven to 375°F. Bake until bread is browned and loaf sounds hollow when tapped, about 45 to 50 minutes. Remove from oven and brush top with butter. Remove from pan and let cool completely on rack before slicing.

Supper Bread

Makes 4 loaves

1¼ cups lukewarm water (90°F)
2 yeast cakes
½ teaspoon firmly packed brown sugar
1 egg, separated

5 tablespoons solid vegetable shortening
3 tablespoons molasses
3 tablespoons honey
1½ teaspoons salt

1 cup lukewarm milk (90°F)
2 tablespoons fresh orange juice
4 cups whole wheat flour, sifted
2½ cups all purpose flour, sifted
¼ teaspoon cumin

Cornmeal
¼ cup water
Butter, room temperature

Grease large bowl and set aside. Combine 1¼ cups lukewarm water, yeast and brown sugar in medium bowl. Mash yeast until dissolved. Let stand until bubbly, about 5 minutes. Stir yolk into yeast mixture.

Combine shortening, molasses, honey and salt in large bowl of electric mixer. Add milk and mix until thoroughly incorporated. Cool 5 minutes. Mix in orange juice. Blend in yeast mixture. Mix in 2 cups whole wheat flour and 1½ cups all purpose flour. Beat at medium-low speed 1 minute. Add remaining flours and continue beating 2 minutes. Blend in cumin. Turn dough out onto lightly floured surface and knead until smooth and elastic, 5 to 6 minutes. Transfer dough to prepared bowl, turning to coat entire surface. Cover with dry cloth and let rise in warm draft-free area until doubled in volume, about 1 hour. Punch dough down. Cover and let rise again until almost doubled, about 30 minutes.

Divide dough into fourths. Shape into oval loaves. Cover loaves and let rise in warm draft-free area 15 minutes.

Preheat oven to 400°F. Heat 2 baking sheets. Dust with cornmeal. Carefully transfer loaves to hot baking sheets. Slash tops diagonally at 3-inch intervals with sharp knife. Beat ¼ cup water and egg white. Brush over top of each loaf. Bake

15 minutes. Reduce oven temperature to 350°F and continue baking until loaves are browned and sound hollow when tapped on bottom, about 25 minutes. Cool slightly on racks. Spread top of each loaf with butter. Serve warm; or cool completely, wrap with plastic and store at room temperature.

West Indian Dark Bread

Makes 2 loaves

1½ cups warm water (105°F to 115°F)
1 envelope dry yeast
¾ cup milk
5 tablespoons butter
¼ cup sugar
1 tablespoon salt
¼ cup molasses
2 cups whole wheat flour
5 to 5¼ cups all purpose flour

Cracked rye flakes

Lightly grease large bowl. Pour warm water into another large bowl. Stir in yeast; set aside. Combine milk, butter, sugar and salt in medium saucepan over medium heat and cook, stirring occasionally, just until sugar dissolves. Blend in molasses. Let cool. Stir milk mixture into dissolved yeast. Add 2 cups whole wheat flour and 2 cups all purpose flour and beat until smooth. Add another 3 cups all purpose flour and mix until soft dough forms, adding remaining flour as necessary. Turn dough out onto lightly floured surface and knead until smooth and elastic, about 8 to 10 minutes. Transfer dough to prepared bowl, turning to coat all surfaces. Cover with towel. Let dough stand in warm draft-free area until doubled in volume.

Generously grease 2 large baking sheets (at least 18 inches diagonally). Punch dough down. Divide in half. Cover with towel and let rest 10 minutes. Transfer dough to prepared sheets. Shape each into 18-inch baguette. Cover with towels and let stand in warm draft-free area until doubled in volume, about 1 hour.

Preheat oven to 400°F. Sprinkle top of each loaf with cracked rye flakes. Bake until loaves are brown and sound hollow when tapped, about 20 to 25 minutes. Cool on rack before slicing.

Anadama Bread (Cornmeal Bread)

Makes two 9 × 5-inch loaves

2½ cups milk
½ cup molasses
¼ cup vegetable oil
1 tablespoon salt

2 envelopes dry yeast
2 cups gluten flour
2¾ to 3¼ cups whole wheat flour

1 cup yellow cornmeal

Scald milk. Measure 2 cups into large bowl. Blend in molasses, oil and salt.

Cool remaining milk to lukewarm and dissolve yeast in it. When molasses mixture is cool, add yeast, gluten flour and 1 cup whole wheat flour and stir well. Cover with damp cloth and let rise in warm draft-free area 1 hour.

Stir in remaining whole wheat flour and cornmeal to make stiff dough. Turn out onto floured board and knead 5 to 6 minutes. Transfer to oiled bowl. Cover and let rise in warm draft-free area until doubled in bulk.

Oil two 9 × 5-inch loaf pans. Shape dough into 2 loaves. Place in pans, cover and let rise in warm draft-free area 30 minutes.

About 15 minutes before baking, preheat oven to 375°F. Bake loaves until golden brown, about 40 minutes. Transfer to racks to cool before slicing.

Maple Oatmeal Bread

Makes one 9 × 5-inch loaf

1 envelope dry yeast
¼ teaspoon sugar
⅔ cup warm water (105°F to 115°F)

2½ cups bread flour
½ cup whole wheat flour
⅓ cup rolled oats

⅓ cup maple syrup
¼ cup instant nonfat dry milk
2 tablespoons (¼ stick) unsalted butter, room temperature
1 teaspoon salt

Rolled oats

Oil large mixing bowl and set aside. Combine yeast and sugar with warm water in small bowl and let stand until proofed, about 10 to 12 minutes.

Combine 2¼ cups bread flour and next 6 ingredients in processor fitted with steel knife and mix about 10 seconds, stopping machine once to scrape down sides of bowl. With machine running, pour yeast mixture through feed tube and blend until dough forms ball, about 40 seconds. If dough is too wet, mix in remaining bread flour 1 teaspoon at a time until no longer sticky. Transfer to oiled bowl, turning to coat all surfaces. Cover bowl with damp towel. Let stand in warm draft-free area until doubled in volume, about 1 hour (an oven preheated to lowest setting for 2 minutes and then turned off works well; be sure to cushion bottom of bowl with pot holder).

Butter 9 × 5-inch loaf pan and sprinkle with oats. Transfer dough to lightly floured surface and roll into rectangle. Roll up lengthwise, pinching ends and seam tightly. Arrange loaf seam side down in prepared pan. Cover with damp towel. Let stand in warm draft-free area until almost doubled in volume, about 45 minutes.

Position rack in center of oven and preheat to 375°F. Bake until bread is golden brown and sounds hollow when tapped on bottom, about 35 to 40 minutes. Remove from pan and let cool on wire rack before slicing.

Mixed Grain Bread Loaves

Makes 1 large loaf and 8 small loaves

2 envelopes dry yeast
2½ cups (or more) warm water (105°F to 115°F)
1 teaspoon honey

4 cups (or more) all purpose flour
3 teaspoons salt

1 tablespoon vegetable oil
4 cups whole wheat flour
½ cup unprocessed bran flakes
½ cup mixed-grain cereal

1 egg blended with 1 tablespoon cream (glaze)

Sprinkle yeast over 1 cup warm water in large measuring cup. Add honey and stir to dissolve. Let stand until foamy, about 5 minutes.

Combine 2 cups all purpose flour and 1½ teaspoons salt in processor. Stir 1½ cups warm water and oil into yeast mixture. With machine running, pour 1 cup yeast mixture through feed tube and blend 30 seconds. Add 2 cups whole wheat flour, ¼ cup bran and ¼ cup mixed-grain cereal. With machine running, add ¼ cup more yeast mixture through feed tube. Blend until dough forms ball, adding more warm water if dough is too dry or more all purpose flour if too sticky. Remove from processor. Repeat with remaining ingredients except glaze.

Grease large bowl. Knead doughs together on lightly floured surface. Place in prepared bowl, turning to coat entire surface. Cover bowl with damp towel. Let dough rise in warm area until doubled, about 1¼ hours.

Grease one 9 × 5-inch loaf pan and eight 2¼ × 4-inch loaf pans. Punch dough down. Knead on lightly floured surface until smooth, about 2 minutes.

Divide dough in half. Shape 1 piece into loaf and place in large pan. Cut remaining dough into 8 pieces, form into loaves and place in small pans. Cover pans with damp towel. Let rise in warm draft-free area until almost doubled in volume, about 1 hour.

Preheat oven to 350°F. Brush loaves with glaze. Bake until loaves sound hollow when tapped on bottom, about 35 minutes for small and 45 minutes for large. Invert onto racks and cool.

Bran Molasses Sunflower Bread

Makes 2 loaves

1½ cakes fresh yeast
¾ cup lukewarm water (95°F)
2 tablespoons sugar

⅓ cup molasses
¼ cup (½ stick) unsalted butter, room temperature
1½ cups milk, scalded and cooled to lukewarm (95°F)

6 to 7 cups unbleached all purpose flour or bread flour
1¼ cups unprocessed bran flakes
½ cup sunflower seeds
1 tablespoon salt

Crumble yeast into small bowl. Stir in lukewarm water and sugar. Let stand until foamy, about 10 minutes.

Meanwhile, add molasses and butter to milk and stir until butter melts. Combine 2 cups all purpose flour, bran, seeds and salt in large bowl. Whisk in yeast and milk mixtures until smooth, about 3 minutes. Using wooden spoon, mix in all purpose flour ½ cup at a time until dough forms soft mass. Knead on heavily floured surface until smooth and satiny, kneading in more flour if sticky.

Grease large bowl. Add dough, turning to coat entire surface. Cover bowl with plastic. Let rise in warm draft-free area until doubled, about 1½ hours.

Grease two 9 × 5-inch loaf pans. Gently knead dough on lightly floured surface until deflated. Cut in half. Pat each piece out into rectangle. Roll up jelly roll fashion, pinching seams to seal. Place seam side down in prepared pans. Cover with towel and let rise in warm draft-free area until doubled in volume, about 45 minutes.

Position rack in center of oven and preheat to 375°F. Bake until loaves pull away from sides of pans, about 45 minutes. Immediately remove from pans. Cool completely on racks.

Red River Cereal Bread

Red River Cereal, a mixture of cracked wheat, rye and flax seed, originated in Manitoba's Red River Valley. If it is unavailable, use a five-grain cereal or quick-cooking oats instead.

Makes two 9 × 5-inch loaves

2 cups boiling water
1 cup Red River Cereal, five-grain cereal or quick-cooking oats
3 tablespoons pure maple syrup or honey
2 tablespoons (¼ stick) unsalted butter
2 teaspoons salt

2 yeast cakes or 2 envelopes dry yeast

2 teaspoons sugar
½ cup warm water (105°F to 115°F)

3 to 3½ cups bread flour
1½ cups whole wheat flour
½ cup unprocessed bran flakes

Cornmeal

1 egg beaten with ½ teaspoon salt (glaze)

Mix 2 cups boiling water, cereal, maple syrup, butter and salt in large bowl until butter melts. Cool to lukewarm.

Dissolve yeast and sugar in ½ cup warm water. Let stand until foamy, about 5 minutes. Stir into cereal.

Combine 3 cups bread flour, whole wheat flour and bran in bowl. Beat into cereal mixture, 1 cup at a time, until smooth. Add enough remaining bread flour to make soft, moist dough. Turn out into lightly floured surface and knead until smooth and elastic, about 10 minutes. (Dough can also be made with heavy-duty electric mixer.)

Butter large bowl. Add dough, turning to coat entire surface. Cover bowl with plastic wrap and towel. Let dough rise in warm draft-free area until doubled in volume, about 1½ hours.

Butter two 9 × 5-inch loaf pans. Dust with cornmeal. Punch dough down and divide in half. Roll each half into rectangle; then roll up, starting at 1 long edge, to form loaves. Place seam side down in prepared pans. Cover with buttered plastic wrap. Let rise in warm draft-free area until doubled, about 45 minutes.

Preheat oven to 400°F. Brush loaves with glaze. Bake until loaves are golden brown and sound hollow when tapped on bottom, about 50 minutes. Turn loaves out of pans onto racks and cool completely before slicing.

Variations
For individual loaves: Bake in twelve 2½ × 4-inch loaf pans about 25 minutes.
For baguettes: Form dough into 3 long loaves. Bake 35 to 40 minutes.
For round loaves: Form dough into 2 round loaves. Bake about 45 minutes.

Sarah's Not Kneaded Bread

Makes two 9 × 5-inch loaves

2 teaspoons dry yeast
3½ cups warm water (105°F to 115°F)
½ cup honey
¼ cup (½ stick) butter, melted and cooled
1 teaspoon salt

1 cup unbleached all purpose flour
6 cups whole wheat flour
1 cup 9-grain cereal
¼ cup sesame seeds
¼ cup sunflower seeds

Cornmeal

Sprinkle yeast onto water in large bowl; add honey and stir to dissolve. Let stand until foamy, 5 minutes.

Mix butter and salt into yeast. Stir in flours 1 cup at a time, using wooden spoon. Thoroughly mix in cereal and seeds. Cover bowl with damp towel. Let rise in warm draft-free area until doubled in volume, about 2¼ hours.

Preheat oven to 350°F. Grease two 9 × 5-inch loaf pans and sprinkle with cornmeal. Stir dough down. Spread evenly in pans. Bake until loaves are brown and sound hollow when tapped on bottom, about 1½ hours. Turn out onto racks. Cool completely.

Shredded Wheat Molasses Bread

Makes two 9 × 5-inch loaves

⅓ cup sugar
⅓ cup unsulfured dark molasses
3 tablespoons unsalted butter, cut into pieces
2 regular-size shredded wheat biscuits, crumbled
1 teaspoon salt

2 cups boiling water
½ cup warm water (105°F to 115°F)
2 envelopes dry yeast
Pinch of sugar
6 cups all purpose flour

Melted butter

Lightly grease large mixing bowl and two 9 × 5-inch loaf pans. Combine sugar, molasses, butter, shredded wheat and salt in large bowl of electric mixer. Pour in boiling water and stir through. Let cool to room temperature, 25 minutes.

Combine warm water, yeast and sugar in small bowl and let stand until foamy and proofed, about 10 minutes. Stir yeast into shredded wheat mixture. Add flour and beat with electric mixer 5 minutes. Turn dough out onto lightly floured surface and knead 5 minutes. Form into ball. Transfer to prepared bowl, turning to coat entire surface. Cover with plastic wrap and damp towel and let rise in warm draft-free area until doubled, about 50 to 60 minutes.

Punch dough down and divide in half. Shape into 2 loaves. Transfer to prepared pans, turning to coat surfaces. Let stand in warm draft-free area until doubled, about 30 to 40 minutes.

Preheat oven to 350°F. Bake until loaves sound hollow when tapped, about 40 to 50 minutes. Turn loaves out onto rack and immediately brush tops with melted butter. Let cool before slicing and serving.

Whole Wheat Seed Bread

Makes two 9 × 5-inch loaves

2 cups warm water (110°F)
2 envelopes dry yeast
2 tablespoons honey
1 cup unbleached all purpose flour
1 cup whole wheat flour

2½ cups whole wheat flour
½ cup yellow cornmeal
½ cup hot water (115°F)

⅓ cup molasses
2 tablespoons corn oil
2 teaspoons salt
1¼ cups shelled raw sunflower seeds
¼ cup poppy seeds
¼ cup sesame seeds
1½ cups unbleached all purpose flour

Grease two 9 × 5-inch glass loaf pans. Grease large bowl and set aside. Combine warm water, yeast and honey in another large bowl and stir until yeast dissolves. Whisk in 1 cup unbleached all purpose flour and 1 cup whole wheat flour. Let stand until light and bubbly, about 30 minutes.

Add 2½ cups whole wheat flour, cornmeal, hot water, molasses, corn oil and salt and mix well. Stir in sunflower, poppy and sesame seeds. Mix in 1½ cups unbleached all purpose flour. Turn dough out onto lightly floured surface and knead until very elastic, about 10 minutes. Transfer dough to greased bowl, turning to coat entire surface. Cover with plastic wrap. Let rise in warm draft-free area until doubled in volume, about 35 minutes. Punch dough down and let rise until doubled, about 30 minutes.

Transfer dough to lightly floured surface and divide in half. Pat each piece into oval. Roll dough pieces up loosely, as for jelly roll, and arrange seam side down in prepared pans. Let rise until almost doubled.

Preheat oven to 375°F. Bake until loaves sound hollow when tapped on bottom, about 40 to 45 minutes. Remove loaves from pans and cool on rack before slicing.

Sprouted Wheat Bread

Makes two 9 × 5-inch loaves

2 envelopes dry yeast
2 cups warm water (105°F to 115°F)
⅓ cup molasses
7 cups whole wheat flour

¼ cup vegetable oil
2 cups sprouted wheat
1 scant tablespoon salt

Dissolve yeast in water in large bowl. Stir in molasses and 2 cups flour and beat 3 to 4 minutes. Cover bowl with damp cloth and let stand in warm draft-free area for 1 hour.

Oil large bowl and set aside. Stir down sponge. Add oil, sprouted wheat, 4½ cups flour and salt and stir well. Sprinkle work surface with remaining ½ cup flour. Turn dough out and knead 7 to 8 minutes, adding more flour if necessary. Transfer to oiled bowl, turning to coat entire surface. Cover with plastic wrap and let stand in warm draft-free area until doubled.

Oil two 9 × 5-inch loaf pans. Punch dough down and divide in half. Shape each half into loaf and place in prepared pans. Let rise about 45 minutes.

About 15 minutes before baking, preheat oven to 375°F. Bake until loaves are nicely browned, 45 to 50 minutes. Cool slightly in pan, then turn out onto rack and let cool 20 minutes. Wrap tightly in plastic and let stand 1 hour before slicing to soften sprouts in crust.

Wheat Berry Batter Bread

Makes one 8 × 4-inch loaf

½ cup wheat berries*
2½ cups water

2¼ cups all purpose flour
1 envelope dry yeast
1 tablespoon sugar
1 tablespoon vegetable oil

½ teaspoon salt
1 cup warm water (105°F to 115°F)

Cornmeal
1 tablespoon unsalted butter, melted

Combine wheat berries with 2½ cups water in saucepan. Cover and let stand overnight. Bring water to boil, then reduce heat and simmer until berries are tender, about 1½ hours. Drain well. Cover and refrigerate until ready to use. *(This will make about 1½ cups. Use ½ cup in recipe and freeze remaining berries.)*

Combine 1½ cups flour with yeast, sugar, oil and salt in large bowl of electric mixer and blend well. Add warm water and beat at medium speed about 3 minutes. Mix in ½ cup cooked, drained wheat berries. Gradually add remaining flour and beat well. Cover and let rise in warm, draft-free area until doubled, about 1 hour.

Preheat oven to 375°F. Generously grease 8 × 4-inch loaf pan and sprinkle with cornmeal. Stir batter down. Turn into loaf pan and bake until bread is well browned, about 1 hour. Brush top with butter. Remove from pan and let cool slightly on rack before slicing.

*Available at natural foods stores.

2 ❧ Rye Breads

To many people a hearty rye loaf represents the pinnacle of the baker's art. If you are accustomed to thinking of rye bread as having two variations—with seeds and without—you may be surprised by all the versions presented here.

Are you tempted by Parmesan Onion Rye spread with sweet butter, Sour Dill Rye ham sandwiches, Peanut Butter Rye studded with nut bits? These are only a few of the possibilities.

Keep in mind that rye behaves somewhat differently from wheat. The higher the proportion of rye flour, the stickier the dough will be. Do not be tempted to add too much flour to counteract the stickiness, or your bread will be heavy and dense. But do be sure to knead thoroughly, because the gluten in rye takes longer to develop properly; without a well developed network of gluten strands the bread will not rise to its fullest.

To give it a perfect mini-environment for rising, try placing the bowl of dough into a larger bowl containing several cups of hot tap water, then covering both bowls with a sheet of plastic wrap. Set the dough in a warm place to rise as usual; the humidity and insulating effect of the water bath will assure an optimum rise and give you extra-professional results.

Beer Barrel Rye

Beer adds rich flavor to this traditional rye. Try it in a sandwich with spicy salami and homemade mayonnaise.

Makes two 1-pound baguettes

2 12-ounce bottles beer
2 tablespoons sugar
2 envelopes dry yeast
4 cups (about) all purpose flour
2 tablespoons honey
1 tablespoon vegetable oil
1 tablespoon salt

1 teaspoon caraway seeds
2 cups rye flour

1 egg blended with 1 tablespoon water and ¼ teaspoon salt (optional glaze)

Oil large bowl and set aside. Grease 2 baking sheets. Bring beer to boil in large saucepan. Reduce heat and simmer 5 minutes *(do not let beer boil over)*. Remove from heat. Pour 2 cups beer into large mixing bowl; discard remainder. Add sugar and stir until dissolved. Cool to 110°F. Sprinkle with yeast. Set aside until foamy, about 5 minutes. Using whisk or fork, beat in 2 cups all purpose flour and honey to form smooth batter. Add oil, salt and caraway seeds and beat well. Mix in rye flour and beat thoroughly. Using hands or wooden spoon, gradually work in remaining all purpose flour, adding only enough to form sticky but workable dough. When dough forms ball, knead briefly in bowl. Turn dough out onto lightly floured surface and knead 10 minutes, dusting with flour as necessary. Transfer dough to oiled bowl, turning to coat entire surface. Cover bowl with plastic wrap and towel. Let stand in warm draft-free area until doubled in volume, about 1 hour.

Turn dough out and knead lightly 2 minutes. Divide dough in half and form into 2 long, narrow loaves. Place each loaf diagonally on prepared baking sheet and brush with egg glaze if desired. Drape loosely with greased waxed paper. Let stand in warm draft-free area until doubled in volume, about 40 to 45 minutes.

Preheat oven to 375°F. Bake until loaves sound hollow when tapped, about 25 to 30 minutes. Transfer to racks to cool completely before slicing.

Craggy Dark Bread

Makes one 2-pound or two 1-pound round loaves

1 cup warm water (105° to 115°F)
¼ cup firmly packed brown sugar
2 envelopes dry yeast
4 eggs, room temperature
¼ cup molasses
1 teaspoon instant coffee powder
3½ to 4 cups all purpose flour
2 tablespoons unsweetened cocoa powder

1 tablespoon salt
1½ cups rye flour
½ cup cornmeal

1 egg blended with 1 tablespoon water
Coarse salt (optional)

Oil large bowl and set aside. Grease 1 or 2 large baking sheets. Combine warm water and brown sugar in large mixing bowl and stir until sugar is dissolved. Sprinkle with yeast. Set aside until foamy, about 5 minutes. Using whisk or fork, blend in eggs, molasses and coffee powder. Add 2 cups all purpose flour, cocoa powder and salt and beat until smooth. Using wooden spoon, mix in rye flour and cornmeal and beat thoroughly. Gradually work in remaining 1½ to 2 cups all purpose flour, adding only enough to form sticky but workable dough. When dough forms ball, knead briefly in bowl. Turn dough out onto lightly floured surface and knead 10 minutes, dusting with flour as necessary. Transfer dough to oiled bowl, turning to coat entire surface. Cover bowl with plastic wrap and towel. Let stand in warm draft-free area until doubled, about 1 hour.

Turn dough out and knead lightly 2 minutes. Form into 1 large round or divide dough in half and form 2 rounds. Transfer to prepared baking sheet(s). Brush with egg glaze. Sprinkle with coarse salt if desired. Drape loosely with greased waxed paper. Set in warm draft-free area until doubled in volume, about 45 minutes.

Preheat oven to 375°F. Bake until bread sounds hollow when tapped, about 35 to 40 minutes for large loaf and 25 to 30 minutes for smaller loaves. Transfer to wire racks and let cool completely before slicing.

Four-Grain Dieter's Bread

Makes two 8¹/₂ × 4¹/₂-inch loaves; 61 calories per ³/₈-inch slice (1 ounce)

2³/₄ cups boiling water
1 cup cracked wheat or bulgur

2 envelopes dry yeast
¹/₄ cup warm water (105°F to 115°F)

1 cup uncooked regular or quick-cooking oats
1 cup dark rye flour
³/₄ cup nonfat dry milk powder

¹/₂ cup soy flour
3 tablespoons dark molasses
1 tablespoon caraway seeds
2 teaspoons salt
3¹/₂ to 4 cups bread flour or unbleached all purpose flour

Milk
2 tablespoons sesame seeds

Pour boiling water over cracked wheat in large bowl. Cool completely.

Sprinkle yeast over warm water; stir to dissolve. Let stand 5 minutes.

Stir oats, rye flour, milk powder, soy flour, molasses, caraway seeds and salt into cracked wheat. Blend in yeast mixture. Gradually mix in 3 to 3¹/₂ cups bread flour until stiff dough forms. Sprinkle work surface generously with some of remaining flour. Turn dough out onto surface and knead until smooth and elastic, about 10 minutes, adding more flour if sticky. Generously grease large bowl. Add dough, turning to coat entire surface. Cover and let rise in warm draft-free area until doubled, about 1 hour.

Grease two 8¹/₂ × 4¹/₂-inch loaf pans. Punch dough down. Divide in half. Shape into 2 loaves. Place in prepared pans. Cover and let rise in warm draft-free area until doubled in volume, approximately 45 minutes.

Preheat oven to 350°F. Brush loaves with milk. Sprinkle with sesame seeds. Using sharp knife, make lengthwise shallow slash down center of each loaf. Bake until loaves pull away from sides of pans and sound hollow when tapped, 40 to 45 minutes. Turn out onto racks. Cool completely.

Fennel Rye Bread

If your food processor is larger than standard size, this recipe can be doubled (do not double the yeast, however).

Makes 2 baguettes

Glaze
1 egg
¹/₂ teaspoon salt

Bread
1 cup warm water (105°F to 115°F)
1 envelope dry yeast
1 tablespoon dark molasses

2 cups (about) bread flour
²/₃ cup rye flour
¹/₄ cup dry milk powder
1¹/₂ teaspoons salt
1 teaspoon fennel seeds

1 tablespoon cornmeal

For glaze: Insert steel knife into processor and mix egg with salt 2 seconds; remove and set aside. Do not clean work bowl.

For bread: Oil large mixing bowl and set aside. Combine warm water, yeast and molasses in small bowl and let stand until foamy, about 10 minutes.

Combine 1¾ cups bread flour, rye flour, powdered milk, salt and fennel in processor work bowl. With machine running, add yeast mixture through feed tube and mix until dough is uniformly moist and elastic, about 40 seconds. If dough is too wet, add remaining bread flour 1 tablespoon at a time and continue mixing until dough is correct consistency. Transfer to oiled bowl, turning to coat all surfaces. Cover bowl with damp towel. Let stand in warm draft-free area (an oven preheated to lowest setting 2 minutes and then turned off works well; cushion bottom of bowl with pot holder) until dough has doubled in volume, about 1 hour.

Grease or oil double French bread pan or baking sheets and sprinkle with cornmeal. Punch dough down and divide in half. Roll 1 half out on lightly floured surface into 8 × 10-inch rectangle. Roll up lengthwise (as for jelly roll), pinching ends and seam tightly. Repeat with remaining dough. Place dough in pans (or on baking sheet) seam side down. Cover lightly with damp towel and let stand in warm draft-free area until doubled in volume, about 45 minutes.

About 15 minutes before baking, position rack in lower third of oven and preheat to 375°F. Slash tops of loaves and brush with glaze, being careful not to drip glaze onto pan. Bake until loaves are deeply colored and sound hollow when tapped on bottom, about 25 to 30 minutes. Remove loaves from pans and let cool on wire rack.

Parmesan Onion Rye

The zest of Parmesan cheese and onion plus a freckling of poppy seeds make this the perfect cocktail bread. It is also a wonderful accompaniment for meals, served with butter or cream cheese.

Makes two 1½-pound loaves

1 teaspoon cornmeal
1½ cups warm water (105°F to 115°F)
1 tablespoon sugar
2 envelopes dry yeast

2 tablespoons (¼ stick) butter
1 cup chopped onion
2 eggs, room temperature
2 tablespoons honey
4 cups (about) all purpose flour

1 tablespoon salt
2 cups rye flour
1 cup freshly grated Parmesan cheese (about 4 ounces)
2 tablespoons poppy seeds

1 egg blended with 1 tablespoon water and ¼ teaspoon salt
Additional poppy seeds (optional)

Oil large bowl and set aside. Grease two 9 × 5-inch loaf pans and sprinkle each with ½ teaspoon cornmeal. Combine warm water and sugar in large mixing bowl and stir until sugar is dissolved. Sprinkle with yeast. Set aside until foamy, about 5 minutes.

Melt butter in skillet over medium-high heat. Add onion and stir until limp and golden, about 5 to 7 minutes; remove from heat. Add 2 eggs and honey to yeast mixture and beat with whisk or fork to combine. Beat in 2 cups all purpose flour with salt and onion. Add rye flour, Parmesan and 2 tablespoons poppy seeds, stirring with wooden spoon until batter is thick. Gradually work in remaining all purpose flour, adding only enough to form sticky but workable dough. When dough forms ball, knead briefly in bowl. Turn dough out onto lightly floured surface and knead 10 minutes, dusting with flour as necessary. Transfer dough to oiled bowl, turning to coat entire surface. Cover bowl with plastic wrap and towel. Let stand in warm draft-free area until doubled, about 1 hour.

Turn dough out and knead lightly 2 minutes. Divide dough in half and form into 2 loaves. Transfer to prepared pans (should be ⅔ full). Brush tops with egg glaze. Sprinkle with additional poppy seeds if desired. Cover pans loosely with greased waxed paper. Let stand in warm draft-free area until doubled in volume, about 45 minutes.

Position rack in center of oven and preheat to 375°F. Bake until loaves sound hollow when tapped, about 30 minutes. Turn out onto wire racks and let cool completely before slicing.

Peanut Butter Rye

Extra-chunky peanut butter gives this loaf both flavor and texture—crunchy peanut bits scattered throughout replace the more traditional seeds.

Makes 2 baguettes

1 teaspoon cornmeal	4 cups (about) all purpose flour
2 cups warm water (105°F to 115°F)	2½ teaspoons salt
2 tablespoons sugar	2 cups rye flour
2 envelopes dry yeast	
½ cup extra-chunky peanut butter	1 egg blended with 1 tablespoon water and ¼ teaspon salt (optional glaze)
1 tablespoon honey	

Oil large bowl and set aside. Grease 2 baking sheets and sprinkle each with ½ teaspoon cornmeal. Combine warm water and sugar in large mixing bowl and stir until sugar is dissolved. Sprinkle with yeast. Set aside until foamy, about 5 minutes. Using whisk or fork, beat peanut butter and honey into yeast mixture. Add 2 cups all purpose flour with salt and beat until smooth. Mix in rye flour, blending thoroughly. Using hands or wooden spoon, gradually work in remaining all purpose flour, adding only enough to form sticky but workable dough. When dough forms ball, knead briefly in bowl. Turn dough out onto lightly floured surface and knead 10 minutes, dusting with flour as necessary. Transfer dough to oiled bowl, turning to coat entire surface. Cover with plastic wrap and towel. Let dough stand in warm draft-free area until doubled in volume, about 1 hour.

Turn dough out and knead lightly 2 minutes. Divide dough in half and form into 2 long, narrow loaves. Place each loaf diagonally on prepared baking sheet. Brush tops with egg glaze if desired. Drape loosely with greased waxed paper. Let dough stand in warm draft-free area until doubled, about 45 minutes.

Preheat oven to 375°F. Bake until loaves sound hollow when tapped, about 25 to 30 minutes. Transfer to racks to cool completely before slicing.

Peasant Bread

A hearty rye bread made without shortening. Makes delicious toast.

Makes 2 medium loaves

2 envelopes dry yeast	½ cup rolled oats
2¼ cups warm potato water* (105°F to 115°F)	1 tablespoon salt
2 cups whole wheat flour	1½ cups dark or light rye flour
1 cup gluten flour	Additional whole wheat flour (about ¾ cup)
⅓ cup molasses	
1 cup unprocessed bran flakes (not cereal)	Rolled oats

Dissolve yeast in warm potato water in large mixing bowl. Stir in 2 cups whole wheat flour, gluten flour and molasses to make sponge. Beat with mixer or by hand several minutes. Cover and let rise in warm draft-free area about 40 minutes.

Stir bran, oats and salt into batter and work in rye flour to make sticky dough. Turn out onto surface generously dusted with whole wheat flour and knead 10 minutes, working in additional flour to make dough stiff but elastic. Transfer to oiled bowl and cover with damp cloth. Let rise in warm draft-free area until doubled, 1 to 1½ hours.

Oil two 9 × 5-inch pans or large baking sheet. Punch dough down and shape into 2 loaves. Roll in oats. Place in baking pans or on sheet. Cover and let rise again until doubled, about 40 minutes.

About 15 minutes before baking, preheat oven to 350°F. Bake loaves until well browned, about 45 minutes. Transfer to racks to cool before slicing.

*Water in which potatoes have been boiled. It is rich in starch and aids the rising.

Quick Rye Bread

This rapidly assembled rye bread has the texture of a kneaded dough, yet it requires only two minutes to mix and one minute of beating by hand.

Makes one 9 × 5-inch loaf

1 envelope dry yeast
½ cup warm water (105°F to 115°F)

½ cup milk, scalded and cooled to lukewarm
2 tablespoons firmly packed brown sugar
2 tablespoons (¼ stick) unsalted butter or margarine

1 teaspoon salt
1⅔ cups bread flour
1 cup rye flour
1 tablespoon caraway seeds

Additional milk and caraway seeds

Sprinkle yeast over warm water and let proof until foamy, about 10 minutes.

Pour cooled milk over brown sugar, butter and salt in large mixing bowl. Add yeast, ¾ cup bread flour, ½ cup rye flour and caraway seeds and beat at medium speed of electric mixer 2 minutes. Add remaining flours and beat until well blended. Cover and let rise in warm area until doubled, about 1 hour.

Generously grease 9 × 5-inch loaf pan. Preheat oven to 350°F. Stir batter down and beat vigorously with wooden spoon for 1 minute. Turn into prepared pan. Brush with a little milk and sprinkle with caraway. Bake until well browned, about 45 to 50 minutes. Remove from pan and cool on rack before slicing.

Recipe can be doubled.

Alderbrook Norwegian Rye Bread

Makes two 8-inch round loaves

2 envelopes dry yeast
1 cup warm water (105°F to 115°F)
1 cup all purpose flour
1 teaspoon sugar

1 cup warm water (105°F to 115°F)
3½ cups (or more) all purpose flour
1½ cups rye flour
⅔ cup firmly packed dark brown sugar

3½ tablespoons unsulfured dark molasses
3 tablespoons butter, melted
1 tablespoon finely grated orange peel
1 teaspoon salt
1 teaspoon vinegar
Pinch of whole aniseed

Solid vegetable shortening

Soften yeast in 1 cup warm water. Combine flour and sugar in medium bowl. Add yeast mixture, stirring well. Let stand until foamy, about 5 minutes.

Stir in remaining warm water. Transfer mixture to large bowl. Add all remaining ingredients except shortening, stirring until thoroughly combined. Turn out onto well-floured surface and knead until dough is smooth and satiny, adding all purpose flour as necessary, about 25 to 30 minutes.

Lightly grease large bowl with shortening. Add dough, turning to coat all surfaces. Cover with towel and let rise in warm draft-free area until doubled, about 1 hour.

Turn dough out onto well-floured surface and knead until no longer sticky, about 10 minutes. Return to same bowl, coating top lightly with shortening. Cover and let rise until doubled, about 30 minutes.

Divide dough in half. Shape each into an 8-inch round loaf. Transfer loaves to baking sheet. Cover and let rise in warm area until doubled, about 30 minutes.

Preheat oven to 350°F. Bake loaves until lightly browned, about 25 to 30 minutes. Cool on racks before slicing.

Ashton Idaho Rye

This homespun loaf, studded with walnuts and fennel seeds, is named for a tiny town tucked between the Grand Tetons and some of the best potato farms in America. The potato you use could well have come from Ashton.

Makes two 1-pound loaves

1 to 2 large potatoes (to yield 1 cup mashed)

1 teaspoon cornmeal
2 tablespoons sugar
2 envelopes dry yeast

1 egg
2 tablespoons molasses
3 to 4 cups all purpose flour

2 cups rye flour
3/4 cup coarsely chopped walnuts
1 tablespoon salt
1 teaspoon fennel seeds

1 egg blended with 1 tablespoon water and 1/4 teaspoon salt (optional glaze)

Peel potatoes; cut into chunks. Transfer to medium saucepan. Add enough water to cover (at least 2 cups). Bring to boil over medium-high heat. Reduce heat and simmer until potatoes are tender. Drain well; reserve water.

Oil large bowl and set aside. Grease 2 baking sheets and sprinkle each with 1/2 teaspoon cornmeal. Measure 1 1/2 cups hot potato water into large mixing bowl (if less than 1 1/2 cups liquid remains after cooking, add water to make 1 1/2 cups). Cool to 110°F. Mash potatoes and measure 1 cup (reserve remainder for another use). Add sugar to potato water and stir until dissolved. Sprinkle with yeast. Set mixture aside until foamy, about 5 minutes.

Blend mashed potato, egg and molasses into yeast mixture. Using wooden spoon or whisk, mix in 2 cups all purpose flour to form smooth batter. Add rye flour, walnuts, salt and fennel seeds and beat thoroughly. Gradually work in remaining 1 to 2 cups all purpose flour, adding only enough to form sticky but workable dough (amount of flour needed will depend on moisture content of potatoes). When dough forms ball, knead briefly in bowl. Turn dough out onto lightly floured surface and knead 10 minutes, dusting with flour as necessary. Transfer dough to oiled bowl, turning to coat entire surface with oil. Cover with plastic wrap and towel. Let stand in warm draft-free area until doubled in volume, about 1 hour.

Turn dough out and knead lightly 2 minutes. Divide dough in half and form into 2 round loaves. Transfer to prepared baking sheets. Brush tops with egg glaze if desired. Drape loosely with greased waxed paper. Let stand in warm draft-free area until doubled in volume, about 50 to 60 minutes.

Preheat oven to 375°F. Bake until loaves sound hollow when tapped, about 35 minutes. Transfer to racks to cool completely before slicing.

Sour Dill Rye

The perfect bread for ham sandwiches—the flavor of dill pickles is baked right into the loaf.

Makes two 1-pound loaves

1 teaspoon cornmeal
1 cup warm water (105°F to 115°F)
1/4 cup sugar
2 envelopes dry yeast
1 egg
4 cups (about) all purpose flour
3/4 cup brine from any style sour dill pickles, room temperature
1 tablespoon vegetable oil

1 tablespoon dried dillweed
2 teaspoons salt
1 teaspoon dill seeds
2 cups rye flour

1 egg blended with 1 tablespoon water and 1/4 teaspoon salt
Additional dill seeds (optional)

Oil large bowl and set aside. Grease 2 baking sheets and sprinkle each with 1/2 teaspoon cornmeal. Combine warm water and sugar in large mixing bowl and stir until sugar is dissolved. Sprinkle with yeast. Set aside until foamy, about 5 minutes. Using whisk or fork, beat 1 egg and 1 cup all purpose flour into yeast mixture. Stir in brine, oil, dillweed, salt and 1 teaspoon dill seeds. Mix in rye flour, blending thoroughly. Using hands or wooden spoon, gradually work in remaining all purpose flour, adding only enough to form sticky but workable dough. When dough forms ball, knead briefly in bowl. Turn dough out onto lightly floured surface and knead 10 minutes, dusting with flour as necessary. Transfer dough to oiled bowl, turning to coat entire surface. Cover with plastic wrap and towel. Let dough stand in warm draft-free area until doubled in volume, about 1 hour.

Turn dough out and knead lightly 2 minutes. Divide dough in half and form into 2 round loaves. Transfer to prepared baking sheets. Brush tops with egg glaze. Sprinkle with additional dill seeds if desired. Drape loosely with greased waxed paper. Let stand in warm draft-free area until doubled in volume, about 35 to 40 minutes.

Preheat oven to 375°F. Bake until loaves sound hollow when tapped, about 25 to 30 minutes. Transfer to racks to cool completely before slicing.

Sweet Potato Peasant Rye

Sunflower seeds accent the flavor and add texture to this dark loaf.

Makes 1 large round loaf

1 teaspoon cornmeal
2 12-ounce bottles dark beer
1 tablespoon sugar
2 envelopes dry yeast
2 tablespoons honey
2 tablespoons molasses
1 teaspoon instant coffee powder

1 cup mashed cooked sweet potato (9 ounces fresh sweet potato or 8 ounces canned)
3 to 3 1/2 cups all purpose flour

2 tablespoons unsweetened cocoa powder
1 tablespoon salt
3 cups rye flour
1/2 cup roasted or raw sunflower seeds
2 tablespoons sesame seeds

1 egg blended with 1 tablespoon water and 1/4 teaspoon salt
Additional sesame seeds (optional)

Oil large bowl and set aside. Grease deep 2-quart baking dish or soufflé dish and sprinkle with cornmeal. Bring beer to boil in large saucepan. Reduce heat and simmer 5 minutes (*do not let beer boil over*). Remove from heat. Measure 2 cups beer; discard remainder. Pour 1 cup into large mixing bowl, add sugar and stir until dissolved. Cool to 110°F. Sprinkle with yeast. Set aside until foamy, about 5 minutes. Meanwhile, blend honey, molasses, coffee powder and remaining 1 cup beer in another bowl. Cool to 110°F.

Stir honey mixture into yeast. Blend in sweet potato. Using whisk or fork, add 2 cups all purpose flour, cocoa powder and salt and beat until smooth. Using wooden spoon, mix in rye flour, sunflower seeds and 2 tablespoons sesame seeds and beat thoroughly. Gradually work in remaining 1 to 1½ cups all purpose flour, adding only enough to form sticky but workable dough. When dough forms ball, knead briefly in bowl. Turn dough out onto lightly floured surface and knead vigorously 15 minutes, dusting with flour as necessary. Transfer dough to oiled bowl, turning to coat entire surface. Cover with plastic wrap and towel. Let stand in warm draft-free area until doubled, about 1 hour.

Turn dough out and knead lightly 5 minutes. Shape into round loaf. Transfer to prepared dish. Brush top with egg glaze. Sprinkle with additional sesame seeds if desired. Using razor blade or very sharp knife, slash shallow cross in top of loaf. Cover loosely with greased waxed paper. Let stand in warm draft-free area until doubled in volume, about 45 minutes.

Preheat oven to 375°F. Bake until loaf sounds hollow when tapped, about 45 minutes. Turn out onto wire rack to cool completely before slicing.

Spiced Dark Bread with Currants

Moist, chewy and fragrant, this bread is reminiscent of an old-fashioned raisin pumpernickel loaf.

Makes 1 loaf

1¼ cups water
5 tablespoons unsulfured molasses
2 tablespoons (¼ stick) unsalted butter
1 ounce unsweetened chocolate, chopped
2 teaspoons dry yeast

2 cups medium or dark rye flour
1 cup Yogurt Bread Starter,* warmed to room temperature over bowl of lukewarm water (80°F to 90°F)
½ cup rolled oats

1½ teaspoons ground ginger
1½ teaspoons salt
1 teaspoon ground cloves
1 teaspoon cinnamon
2 to 3 cups bread flour

⅔ cup dried currants

Grease large bowl and set aside. Combine water, molasses, butter and chocolate in small saucepan over medium-low heat and warm slowly to 100°F. Blend in yeast. Remove from heat and let stand until bubbly, about 10 to 12 minutes.

Combine rye flour, starter, oats, ginger, salt, cloves, cinnamon and molasses mixture in processor and mix 10 seconds, or until batter is sticky and elastic. Transfer to mixing bowl. Beat in enough bread flour to form stiff, slightly sticky dough. Knead until slightly elastic, about 15 minutes. Transfer dough to prepared bowl, turning to coat all surfaces. Cover with plastic and let stand at room temperature until doubled, about 3 hours.

Generously grease 8-inch springform pan. Punch dough down. Cover and let rise again until doubled in volume, about 2 more hours.

Lightly flour currants, shaking off excess. Stir into dough. Turn dough out onto lightly floured surface and flatten with palms of hands. Shape dough into ball. Arrange in prepared pan and flatten slightly. Cover with towel and let rise again until doubled in volume, about 3 more hours.

Position rack in lower third of oven and preheat to 450°F. Place bread in oven and immediately reduce temperature to 375°F. Bake 40 minutes. Reduce temperature to 325°F and continue baking until bottom of loaf sounds hollow when tapped, about 10 to 15 mintues. Turn out onto rack to cool before slicing.

*Yogurt Bread Starter

Store in the refrigerator, stirring once a week. Each time starter is used, it should be replenished with ½ cup warm water (90°F) and ½ cup rye or whole wheat flour, then covered and allowed to stand in a warm draft-free area until mixture is bubbly. Store covered in the refrigerator for several days to reactivate. Starter requires four days initial preparation.

Makes 2 quarts

2 cups light or medium rye flour
1 cup plain yogurt, room temperature
¾ cup warm water (90°F)
2½ tablespoons apple cider vinegar
1 tablespoon dry yeast
½ teaspoon crushed caraway seeds
½ teaspoon ground cardamom

To be added each of last 3 days:

1 cup light or medium rye flour
2 tablespoons firmly packed brown sugar dissolved in ¾ cup warm water

Combine 2 cups rye flour with yogurt, water, vinegar, yeast, caraway and cardamom in large bowl and beat until well blended. Cover and let stand at warm room temperature for 24 hours.

Beat in 1 cup rye flour with brown sugar mixture. Let stand at warm room temperature another 24 hours.

Repeat procedure with same amount of flour, sugar and warm water. Let stand 12 to 24 hours.

3 ❧ Basic Yeast Rolls, Croissants and Breadsticks

There are times when rolls, yeast buns and other bread "individuals" fit the bill even better than homemade loaves do. A basket of freshly baked breadsticks or handsome croissants on a buffet table is often more convenient than a single large loaf, and homemade hamburger buns are a real attention-getter at picnics and barbecues.

This selection of rolls, buns and other small yeast breads will give you a good idea of the possibilities. The classic, country-style Buttermilk Yeast Biscuits (page 28) and the various dinner rolls—potato, whole wheat, rye, corn—make wonderful partners for hearty soups and main courses. Crescent Rolls and Croissants (pages 29 and 30) are bits of baking wizardry that will show off your skills to the maximum. And A Sheaf of Wheaten Breadsticks (page 34) is a *tour de force* of delicious decorativeness.

In short, the recipes in this chapter will fit in nicely whether the fare is to be simple or sophisticated.

Buttermilk Yeast Biscuits

Makes about 4 dozen

1 envelope dry yeast
2 tablespoons warm water (105°F to 115°F)
5 to 5½ cups sifted all purpose flour
2 tablespoons sugar
1 tablespoon baking powder

1 teaspoon baking soda
1 teaspoon salt
1 cup solid vegetable shortening
2 cups buttermilk

Melted butter

Sprinkle yeast over warm water in small bowl and let stand until dissolved, about 5 minutes. Meanwhile, resift flour with sugar, baking powder, soda and salt into large bowl. Using pastry blender, cut in shortening until mixture resembles coarse meal. Mix in buttermilk and dissolved yeast. Turn dough out onto lightly floured work surface and knead until smooth and soft, about 10 minutes.

Position rack in upper third of oven and preheat to 450°F. Reflour work surface. Roll dough out to thickness of ½ inch. Cut out biscuits using 2-inch cutter. Transfer to ungreased baking sheet, spacing evenly. Brush tops with melted butter. Bake until lightly browned, about 15 minutes. Serve hot. *(Biscuits can be baked 1 day ahead. Reheat in 450°F oven before serving.)*

Potato Rolls

Makes 2 dozen

1 small potato (3 ounces), peeled and halved
1 envelope dry yeast
2 teaspoons sugar

2 cups bread flour
1 cup unbleached all purpose flour
2 tablespoons (¼ stick) unsalted butter

1½ teaspoons salt

1 egg
½ teaspoon salt
Celery seeds, sesame seeds or coarse salt (optional)

Oil large mixing bowl and set aside. Cook potato in small saucepan in enough water to cover until soft. Remove from heat and let stand until water cools to temperature of 105°F to 115°F. Transfer 1 cup water to small bowl. Add yeast and sugar and let stand in warm place until mixture is foamy, about 10 minutes.

Shred potato in processor using light pressure. Leave in work bowl.

Insert steel knife. Add bread flour, ½ cup all purpose flour, butter and salt to work bowl and mix 5 seconds. With machine running, pour yeast mixture through feed tube. Add enough remaining all purpose flour to make dough sticky and soft, but not wet. Process until dough comes away from sides of work bowl and is smooth and elastic, about 30 to 40 seconds.

Oil large bowl. Transfer dough to oiled bowl, turning to coat all surfaces. Cover with damp towel and let stand in warm draft-free area until doubled, about 1 hour.

Generously grease two 12-cup muffin pans and 2 long pieces of plastic wrap. Punch dough down. Transfer to lightly floured board. Divide dough in half and cut each half into 12 equal pieces. Form each piece into smooth, rounded ball, pinching dough on bottom of each roll. Place rolls pinched sides down in pans. Place plastic wrap over rolls greased side down. Let stand in warm draft-free area until doubled, about 1 hour. Discard plastic wrap.

About 15 minutes before baking, preheat oven to 400°F.

Mix egg with salt in processor and use to glaze rolls, being careful not to drip mixture onto pans. Sprinkle with celery seeds, sesame seeds or coarse salt if desired. Bake 10 minutes. Reduce oven temperature to 350°F and continue baking until rolls are lightly browned, about 10 to 12 minutes. Remove rolls from pans immediately; cool on racks.

Crescent Rolls

These rolls are even better made a day or two ahead and recrisped.

Makes 22 to 24

1 cup warm water (105°F to 115°F)
2 tablespoons sugar
1 envelope dry yeast

3 cups unbleached all purpose flour
¼ cup (½ stick) unsalted butter (room temperature), cut into 4 pieces

2 tablespoons instant dry milk powder
1 teaspoon salt

¾ cup (1½ sticks) unsalted butter, room temperature

1 egg

Lightly flour jelly roll pan. Oil large mixing bowl and generously butter 2 baking sheets; set aside.

Combine water, sugar and yeast in small bowl and let proof until foam rises to surface, about 10 minutes.

Using mixer fitted with dough hook: Combine 2½ cups flour, ¼ cup butter, milk and salt and mix until butter is size of small peas. Add dissolved yeast mixture and continue beating until dough is moist, smooth and elastic, adding remaining flour as necessary.

Using food processor: Combine 2½ cups flour, ¼ cup butter, milk and salt and mix 5 seconds. Add half of yeast and combine using on/off turns. Add remaining yeast and process 5 seconds. Add ¼ cup of remaining flour and mix 30 to 40 seconds. *Dough should work away from sides of bowl and mass together on steel knife, but not necessarily form smooth ball. Dough should also be moist and elastic. If necessary, add remaining flour 2 tablespoons at a time and process several seconds longer until texture is correct.*

Transfer dough to oiled bowl and turn to coat entire surface. Cover with damp towel and let stand in warm draft-free area until doubled in size, about 1½ hours. (An oven preheated to lowest setting 2 minutes and then turned off works well. Cushion bottom of bowl with pot holder or folded towel.)

Transfer dough to jelly roll pan and cover with plastic wrap. Press dough evenly into place, using plastic "mitt" to assist. Refrigerate 30 minutes.

Place dough on lightly floured surface and roll into rectangle about 10 × 20 inches. Cover lower ⅔ of dough with remaining ¾ cup butter (which has been pinched off by the inch), leaving 1-inch border around sides and bottom. Fold upper third over buttered portion, bringing lower third over (as you would fold a letter). Turn vertically on board and roll into rectangle 10 × 22 inches, using more flour as needed. Fold again in thirds (this is called a "turn"). Wrap in plastic and chill 30 minutes. Place dough vertically on board and roll and fold again, repeating 1 more "turn" for a total of 3. Wrap dough in plastic and chill in refrigerator for 1 hour.

Cut dough in half. Roll out 1 half to form rectangle 10 × 22 inches. Cut rectangle in half lengthwise. Using croissant or pizza cutter, or tip of sharp knife, cut each half into 6 triangles. (There will be some scraps of leftover dough.) Press a small marble of leftover dough ½ inch in on base of triangles. Fold dough over and roll toward point of triangle into sausage shape, stretching with both hands as it is rolled. Form each roll into "C" shape by bending in edges. Repeat with all triangles and with remaining half of dough.

Space rolls 2 inches apart on baking sheets. Cover with waxed paper and let rise about 1 to 1½ hours at room temperature until they are soft, somewhat puffy and almost doubled in size. *If you have only one oven, bake in 2 batches, refrigerating last batch initially for 10 minutes to retard rising.*

About 15 minutes before baking, position rack in center of oven and preheat to 475°F. Beat egg and brush rolls lightly with glaze, being careful not to drip egg onto baking sheet. Bake 5 minutes. Reduce heat to 400°F and bake for an additional 15 minutes, or until rolls are deep brown.

Crescent rolls can be frozen before baking. Freeze on foil-lined baking sheets and then place in airtight plastic bags. Allow to thaw in refrigerator 24 hours and let rise 1½ hours at room temperature.

For baguette-shaped loaves: Use only 1½ teaspoons sugar and do not use additional ¾ cup butter. After kneading dough, let rise until doubled in bulk. Punch down and let rise again until doubled. Punch down and shape into 2 baguettes. Place in baguette pans or on baking sheets that have been oiled and sprinkled with cornmeal. Let rise again. When dough has doubled, brush with egg and bake at 375°F for 30 minutes.

The Buttery Croissants

Makes about 3 dozen

3 envelopes dry yeast
7 tablespoons sugar
3 cups warm milk (105°F to 115°F)

2 pounds (about 8 cups) unbleached bread flour
1 cup plus 2 tablespoons pastry flour

1 tablespoon salt

2 cups (4 sticks) unsalted butter, room temperature

1 egg
1 tablespoon water

Combine yeast, sugar and milk and let stand until foamy, about 10 minutes.

Measure flours and salt into large bowl of electric mixer. Add yeast and beat at low speed just until ingredients are combined and dough is smooth and slightly sticky. Turn out onto lightly floured baking sheet, cover with plastic wrap and refrigerate for 1 hour.

Dust work surface and dough with flour. Roll out dough into 36 × 12-inch rectangle, making sure corners are square. Brush off excess flour. Leaving 1-inch margin, spread ⅔ of dough (24 × 12-inch portion) with butter. Fold unbuttered part over half of buttered part, then fold over remaining buttered dough. (There will be 2 layers of butter and 3 layers of dough.) Press ends with rolling pin to seal. Place on lightly floured baking sheet, cover and return to refrigerator to rest 20 to 30 minutes.

Roll out dough again into 36 × 12-inch rectangle. Fold in thirds, cover and return to refrigerator to rest another 20 to 30 minutes. Repeat rolling, folding and resting 2 more times. After last folding refrigerate for 2 to 3 hours.

To shape croissants, remove dough from refrigerator and cut in half lengthwise; return half of dough to refrigerator. Roll remaining dough on well-floured work surface until 10 inches wide and ¼ inch thick. Cut in half to make 2 pieces 5 inches wide.

Mark strips into 5-inch triangles. Cut precisely using pastry cutter or pizza wheel. Separate triangles and place on floured tray. Chill. Repeat with remaining half of dough.

Line baking sheet with aluminum foil. Remove 3 or 4 triangles at a time from refrigerator and roll from broad base toward point, stretching as you roll and ending with point on top. Place dough on baking sheet and bend ends inward to form crescent shape. Repeat until baking sheet is filled. Lightly beat egg and water and brush over tops.

Let rise uncovered in warm place (area should not be so warm that butter runs out) until dough is doubled. *(At this point croissants may be frozen. Allow to thaw 1½ to 2 hours before baking.)*

Preheat oven to 450°F. Brush tops again with egg wash. Bake 1 sheet at a time until croissants are golden, about 10 minutes. Transfer to racks to cool.

Whole Wheat Hamburger Buns

Makes 1 dozen

1 **envelope dry yeast**
1¼ **cups warm water (105°F to 115°F)**
½ **cup milk**
¼ **cup (½ stick) butter or margarine, melted**
2 **tablespoons honey**

2 **tablespoons molasses**
1 **teaspoon salt**
2⅓ **cups whole wheat flour**
2 **cups unbleached all purpose flour**

1 **egg white**
1 **tablespoon cold water**

Soften yeast in ¼ cup lukewarm water in large mixing bowl. Using electric mixer, beat in remaining water, milk, melted butter or margarine, honey, molasses and salt. Set aside ⅓ cup whole wheat flour for kneading; beat in remaining flour 1 cup at a time until dough is too stiff for beaters, then beat with spoon. Turn out onto floured board and knead several minutes using remaining whole wheat flour. Transfer to lightly greased bowl, turning to coat entire surface. Cover with damp cloth and let rise in warm area until doubled.

Lightly grease baking sheet. Punch dough down. Using rolling pin, roll out on floured surface to thickness of ¼ inch. Cut into 24 3½-inch rounds, rerolling scraps as necessary. Arrange on baking sheet, cover and let rise for 1 hour.

Preheat oven to 375°F. Beat egg white lightly with water and use to glaze *half* of the rounds (these will be the tops). Bake until golden brown, about 12 to 15 minutes. Cool before using.

Hamburger buns can be frozen.

Whole Wheat Potato Dinner Rolls

Delicious rolls that can be partially baked, then frozen. Finish baking just before serving, for fresh taste.

Makes about 2½ dozen

2 **baking potatoes, peeled and cut into 1-inch pieces**

2 **envelopes dry yeast**
11 **tablespoons butter, room temperature**
½ **cup sugar**
2 **eggs, beaten to blend, room temperature**

2 **teaspoons salt**
1 **cup warm milk (105°F to 115°F)**
5 **cups unbleached all purpose flour**
2 **cups whole wheat flour**

1 **egg blended with 1 tablespoon water (glaze)**

Cook potatoes in boiling water to cover until tender. Drain, reserving cooking liquid. Mash potatoes. Cool potatoes and liquid to 105°F to 115°F.

Measure ½ cup warm potato cooking liquid into small bowl. Sprinkle yeast over; stir to dissolve. Cream butter and sugar using heavy-duty mixer until light and fluffy. Add 1 cup mashed potatoes, eggs and salt and beat until smooth. Blend in yeast and milk. Combine both flours in another bowl. Mix 4½ cups flour into potato mixture, using dough hook. Add remaining flour ½ cup at a time until soft dough forms. Knead dough with mixer until smooth and shiny, about 10 minutes. Knead on lightly floured surface until no longer sticky, about 2 minutes. (Dough can also be mixed by hand.) Butter large bowl. Add dough, turning to coat entire surface. Cover bowl with plastic. Let dough rise in warm draft-free area until doubled in volume, about 2 hours.

Punch dough down. Knead on lightly floured surface until smooth, about 2 minutes. Butter 30 muffin tins. Pinch off 1-inch pieces of dough and roll into rounds between palms. Place 3 in each prepared tin. Brush with glaze. Cover lightly with towel and let rise in warm draft-free area until doubled in volume, about 1 hour.

Preheat oven to 400°F. Bake rolls until golden brown, about 15 minutes. Transfer to racks. *(Can be prepared 1 day ahead. Cool completely. Wrap airtight. Reheat uncovered in 350°F oven about 3 minutes.)* Serve warm.

Variation

For brown and serve rolls, bake until very light brown, about 10 minutes. Transfer to racks and cool completely. Wrap airtight and freeze. Thaw rolls at room temperature. Arrange on baking sheet and bake in 400°F oven until golden brown, about 5 minutes.

Bran English Muffins

Seven-ounce tunafish cans with both ends removed make excellent forms for shaping this dough.

Makes 1 dozen

1 envelope dry yeast or 1 yeast cake
½ cup warm water
½ cup milk, scalded
½ cup boiling water
1 tablespoon honey
2 cups whole wheat flour

1 cup unbleached all purpose flour
½ cup unprocessed bran flakes (not cereal)
1 teaspoon salt
½ teaspoon baking soda

Finely ground yellow cornmeal

Dissolve yeast in warm water and set aside to proof. Mix scalded milk and boiling water in large bowl. Add honey and let stand until lukewarm. Stir in yeast and whole wheat flour. Cover with damp cloth and let stand in warm draft-free area until doubled.

Stir sponge down. Combine all purpose flour, bran, salt and soda and blend into sponge. Turn out onto floured surface and knead well (dough should be workable but sticky). Return dough to bowl and let rise again 25 to 30 minutes.

Grease 12 tuna can "rings." Punch dough down and roll or pat out to ½-inch thickness. Cut into circles and transfer *with rings* to flat surface. Let rise until doubled, about 1 hour.

Dust both sides with cornmeal. Toast on both sides on ungreased griddle until browned, about 6 to 8 minutes per side, removing ring after first side is browned. Let muffins cool on rack. Separate halves with fork. Wrap well and refrigerate. Toast under broiler or in toaster oven just before serving.

Feather Rye Rolls

If you like soft, yeasty rolls with the nutty bite of whole grain, these could become your favorites. They are so light in texture and subtle in flavor that many people mistake them for whole wheat. The dough can also be formed into small loaves.

Makes 36 rolls or six 5½ × 3-inch loaves

2 cups milk
3 tablespoons sugar
2 envelopes dry yeast
4 eggs
5½ to 6 cups all purpose flour
2 cups rye flour
½ cup (1 stick) butter, melted and cooled

¼ cup vegetable oil
2½ teaspoons salt

1 egg blended with 1 tablespoon water and ¼ teaspoon salt (optional glaze)

Oil large bowl and set aside. Grease baking sheets and/or small loaf pans. Scald milk; pour into large mixing bowl and cool to 110°F. Add sugar and stir until dissolved. Sprinkle with yeast. Set aside until foamy, about 5 minutes. Add eggs and beat with whisk or fork just to blend. Add 2 cups all purpose flour and beat until smooth. Using wooden spoon, mix in rye flour, butter, oil and salt and beat thoroughly. Gradually work in remaining 3½ to 4 cups all purpose flour, adding only enough to form sticky but workable dough. When dough forms ball, knead briefly in bowl. Turn dough out onto lightly floured surface and knead 5 minutes, dusting with flour as necessary. Transfer dough to oiled bowl, turning to coat entire surface. Cover with plastic wrap and towel. Let stand in warm draft-free area until doubled, about 1 hour.

Turn dough out and knead lightly 2 minutes. Divide dough into 36 small balls for rolls or 6 equal pieces for loaves. Arrange rolls on prepared baking sheets, spacing 2 inches apart, or transfer dough to prepared loaf pans (pans should be ⅔ full). Brush with egg glaze if desired. Cover loosely with greased waxed paper. Let stand in warm draft-free area until doubled in volume, about 45 minutes.

Preheat oven to 375°F. Bake until bread sounds hollow when tapped, about 20 minutes for rolls and 25 to 30 minutes for loaves. Serve rolls warm; transfer loaves to wire racks and let cool completely before slicing.

Stone-Ground Corn Rolls

Makes about 32

2 cups milk
¾ cup stone-ground cornmeal
½ cup sugar
½ cup solid vegetable shortening
1½ teaspoons salt

2 eggs, beaten
1 envelope dry yeast dissolved in ¼ cup warm water
6 cups unbleached all purpose flour

Grease baking sheets. Combine milk and cornmeal in large saucepan over low heat and cook, stirring frequently, until thick, about 15 minutes. Add sugar, shortening and salt and mix well. Cool to lukewarm. Blend in eggs and yeast. Slowly mix in flour. Knead until smooth, about 12 minutes. Pinch off 1½- to 2-inch diameter balls of dough and arrange on prepared sheets. Let rise in warm draft-free area until doubled, about 1½ to 2 hours.

Preheat oven to 375°F. Bake rolls until golden brown, about 15 minutes. Serve immediately.

A Sheaf of Wheaten Breadsticks

These attractive bread-sticks, each shaped like an individual stalk of wheat, can be used as a graceful edible centerpiece. The flavor and texture of the bread are enhanced by the addition of cornmeal and buckwheat. Shape the "wheat" with a casual hand, bending a few of the stalks to the right, others to the left, so when the grain is finally gathered and stood upright in a handsome basket, the "sheaf" will look full.

Makes 2 dozen

1 cup water
1/3 cup yellow cornmeal

1 1/2 cups warm water (105°F to 115°F)
1 1/2 envelopes dry yeast or 1 yeast cake
1/4 teaspoon sugar

2 tablespoons buckwheat flour
2 teaspoons salt
5 1/4 cups (about) unbleached all purpose flour

1 egg yolk
1 tablespoon water

Bring 1 cup water to boil in saucepan. Stir in cornmeal. Remove from heat and let cool to lukewarm.

Pour 1 1/2 cups warm water into large mixing bowl. Add yeast and sugar, stirring until sugar is dissolved. Add buckwheat flour, salt and cornmeal. Stir in enough unbleached flour to make dough firm enough to knead.

Lightly oil large bowl. Turn dough out onto floured surface and knead about 10 minutes, adding flour as necessary. (Dough should be elastic and firm but not overly stiff.) Place dough in oiled bowl, turning to coat entire surface. Cover with towel and let stand in warm draft-free area 1 hour.

Lightly oil baking sheets. Punch dough down and divide into 24 pieces. Place on unfloured surface and roll each into breadstick 15 to 18 inches long. Fold top 5 inches of stick back against itself so top is doubled. Place sticks fairly close together on baking sheets.

Preheat oven to 350°F. Using small scissors, snip along tops, gently pulling individual "grains" slightly outward. Beat egg yolk with 1 tablespoon water and lightly glaze sticks. Immediately bake sticks (without further rising) until golden brown, about 30 minutes. Serve from basket or gather decoratively and tie with smooth thin rope, ribbon or string.

Fennel Breadsticks

The same pungent seeds that give Italian sausage its distinctive flavor appear here in golden breadsticks.

Makes 1 dozen

1/4 cup warm water (105°F to 115°F)
1 teaspoon dry yeast
1/2 cup beer, room temperature
6 tablespoons olive oil
2 teaspoons fennel seeds
3/4 teaspoon salt

2 to 2 1/2 cups all purpose flour

1 egg beaten with 1 tablespoon water
Coarse salt (optional)

Oil large bowl and set aside. Pour warm water into another large bowl and sprinkle with yeast. Let stand until foamy, about 5 minutes. Add beer, olive oil, fennel seeds and salt to yeast mixture and blend well. Beat in 2 cups flour using mixer or wooden spoon.

Turn dough out onto well-floured surface and knead until smooth and elastic, about 10 minutes, adding more flour 1 tablespoon at a time if dough is sticky. Transfer to prepared bowl, turning to coat entire surface. Cover with plastic wrap and let stand in warm draft-free area until doubled in volume, about 30 minutes.

Preheat oven to 325°F. Line large baking sheet with foil; generously butter foil. Punch dough down, turn out onto work surface and knead briefly. Divide dough into 12 equal pieces. Roll each piece into 9-inch-long cylinder. Arrange on prepared baking sheet. Brush breadsticks with egg mixture. Sprinkle with coarse salt if desired. Bake until evenly browned, about 35 minutes. Serve warm or at room temperature.

4 ❦ Savory Yeast Breads and Rolls

Here is where the fun really begins for bakers who want to expand their bread repertoire well beyond the basics. This chapter features savory breads that are perfect accompaniments to a meal; in the next chapter you will find their sweetened counterparts for breakfast, brunch or teatime.

Flavored breads offer tremendous possibilities to the innovative cook. They are especially appealing when "custom-designed" to complement the main dish. Country ham or thick pork chops, for example, would be splendid with Washington Bread (page 36), which is made with both cornmeal and whole corn kernels. Herbed breads and rolls are marvelous partners for robust stews, while Garlic Foccaccia (page 42) is perfect with pasta. And don't forget that savory breads make exceptional sandwiches: Imagine dill- and caraway-speckled Country Onion Bread (page 39) wrapped around a thick layer of corned beef, or Burgundian Walnut Bread (page 43) topped with something as simple as cream cheese.

Many of these loaves are hearty enough to be virtually the centerpiece of a meal. They make even the lightest snack or supper something terrific.

Washington Bread

Makes one 9 × 5-inch loaf

Glaze
1 egg
½ teaspoon salt

Bread
1 envelope dry yeast
2 teaspoons firmly packed light brown sugar
½ cup plus 2 tablespoons warm water (105°F to 115°F)

3 cups bread flour
1 7-ounce can whole kernel corn, drained
¼ cup yellow cornmeal
1 tablespoon vegetable oil
1 teaspoon salt

Cornmeal

For glaze: Insert steel knife into processor and mix egg with salt 2 seconds; remove and set aside. Do not clean work bowl.

For bread: Oil large mixing bowl and set aside. Combine yeast and sugar with warm water in small bowl and let stand until foamy, about 10 minutes.

Combine 2¾ cups bread flour, corn, cornmeal, oil and salt in processor work bowl and mix about 10 seconds, stopping machine once to scrape down sides of bowl. With machine running, pour yeast mixture through feed tube and mix until dough forms ball, about 40 seconds. If dough is too wet, mix in remaining bread flour 1 teaspoon at a time until no longer sticky. Transfer to oiled bowl, turning to coat all surfaces. Cover bowl with damp towel. Let stand in warm draft-free area until doubled in volume, about 1 hour (an oven preheated to lowest setting for 2 minutes and then turned off works well; cushion bottom of bowl).

Butter 9 × 5-inch loaf pan and sprinkle with cornmeal. Transfer dough to lightly floured surface and roll into rectangle. Roll up lengthwise, pinching ends and seam tightly. Arrange loaf seam side down in prepared pan. Cover with damp towel. Let stand in warm draft-free area until almost doubled in volume, about 35 minutes.

Position rack in center of oven and preheat to 375°F. Brush top of loaf with glaze, being careful not to drip onto pan. Bake until bread is golden brown and sounds hollow when tapped on bottom, about 35 minutes. Remove from pan and cool on rack.

Herb Loaf

Makes one 6 × 3-inch loaf

1¼ to 1½ cups all purpose flour
1 tablespoon sugar
1 teaspoon salt
½ teaspoon dried dillweed
Pinch of dried sage
Pinch of dried marjoram

2 teaspoons dry yeast

⅓ cup milk
⅓ cup water
2 teaspoons butter

Mix ½ cup flour with sugar, salt, dillweed, sage, marjoram and undissolved yeast in large bowl.

Combine milk, water and butter in small saucepan and heat slowly until warm. Add to dry ingredients and beat 2 minutes on medium speed of mixer. Add enough remaining flour to make stiff batter and beat until well blended. Cover with greased waxed paper and let rise in warm draft-free area until doubled in bulk, about 45 minutes.

Fifteen minutes before baking, preheat oven to 375°F. Grease 6 × 3 × 2¼-inch loaf pan. Stir batter down and beat vigorously for about 1 minute. Turn into pan and bake until browned, 30 to 40 minutes. Remove from pan and let cool on rack before slicing.

Herbed Tomato Bread

Makes 1 large round loaf

2 tablespoons olive oil
1/2 cup minced shallots
2 garlic cloves, minced
2 tablespoons chopped fresh basil
1 tablespoon fresh thyme or oregano leaves

3 1/2 teaspoons sugar
1 envelope dry yeast
1/2 cup warm water (105°F to 115°F)

12 ounces tomatoes, peeled, seeded and pureed (1 2/3 cups)
2 teaspoons salt
3 1/2 to 4 1/2 cups unbleached all purpose flour

1 egg beaten with 1 tablespoon water (glaze)
4 fresh thyme or oregano sprigs

Heat olive oil in heavy medium skillet over medium-low heat. Add shallots, cover and cook until translucent, stirring occasionally, about 10 minutes. Add garlic and stir 2 minutes; do not brown. Mix in basil and thyme or oregano. Cool mixture to room temperature.

Sprinkle 1/2 teaspoon sugar and yeast over water in bowl of heavy-duty mixer fitted with dough hook. Stir until yeast dissolves. Cover and let stand until foamy, about 10 minutes.

Coat large bowl with olive oil. Add shallot mixture to yeast. Mix in tomato puree, remaining 3 teaspoons sugar and salt. Add flour 1 cup at a time and blend until dough is soft and smooth and cleans sides of bowl. Knead until elastic, 5 to 7 minutes. (Dough can also be prepared by hand.) Add dough to prepared bowl, turning to coat entire surface. Cover with plastic wrap, then kitchen towel. Let stand in warm draft-free area until doubled, approximately 1 1/2 hours.

Line baking sheet with parchment. Punch dough down. Turn out onto lightly floured surface and knead 2 minutes. Shape dough into large round; flatten slightly. Transfer to prepared sheet. Cover with towel. Let rise in warm draft-free area until almost doubled in volume, 45 minutes.

Position rack in center of oven and preheat to 400°F. Brush loaf with egg glaze. Decorate with herbs. Bake 15 minutes. Reduce oven temperature to 350°F and continue baking until crust is deep russet-orange and loaf sounds hollow when tapped on bottom, about 30 minutes. (If top browns too quickly, cover loosely with foil.) Cool on rack. *(Can be prepared 1 day ahead, wrapped in plastic and stored at room temperature. Reheat in 350°F oven for 5 minutes.)*

Mushroom Bread

This loaf makes terrific toast and is also a tasty partner for canapés and appetizers. The mushroom-shaped version is a whimsical addition to any buffet table. Best made one day ahead as the flavors mellow with standing.

Makes 1 medium loaf

1/4 cup warm water (105°F to 115°F)
3 tablespoons firmly packed light brown sugar
1 envelope dry yeast

3 cups unbleached all purpose flour
3 1/2 ounces Oven Duxelles*
1 medium-size green onion, minced
1 1/8 teaspoons salt

1/2 cup plus 2 tablespoons warm buttermilk (105°F to 115°F)
2 tablespoons (1/4 stick) unsalted butter or margarine, room temperature

1 egg
1/2 teaspoon salt

For mushroom-shaped loaf, grease interior and rim of 12-ounce corn can. Cut cardboard square measuring 2 inches larger than diameter of can. Trace can opening and cut out, discarding center ring. Cover cardboard collar with foil and fit just over open end of can (it should fit tightly). Grease foil generously. Place 6 1/2-cup ring mold under collar to provide extra support.

Combine water, brown sugar and yeast and let stand until foamy and proofed, about 10 minutes.

Oil large bowl and set aside. Combine flour, duxelles, onion, salt and yeast mixture in large mixing bowl. Gradually blend in buttermilk. Work in butter. Turn dough out onto lightly floured surface and knead until smooth and elastic, about 12 minutes. Transfer to oiled bowl, turning to coat entire surface. Cover with damp towel and let stand in warm draft-free area until doubled in volume, about 1 to 1½ hours.

Punch dough down. Shape with hands. Transfer to can and set on baking sheet. Cover loosely with plastic wrap and let stand in warm draft-free area until almost doubled, about 45 minutes.

About 15 minutes before baking, position over rack to lowest level. Cover with unglazed quarry tiles if desired (this will result in a crisper crust). Preheat oven to 400°F. Using fingertips, gently press outer edge of mushroom "cap" down to foil-covered collar. Reshape cap, centering directly over "stem" for balance. Beat egg with salt and use to glaze loaf. Bake 15 minutes. Cover cap with foil and continue baking an additional 40 minutes. Remove from oven and let cool 5 minutes. Turn out of can, cover cap with foil and place bread cap side down on baking sheet. Bake until stem is firm and browned, about 15 minutes. Cool bread on wire rack before slicing.

For regular loaf, use greased 8 × 4½-inch pan and bake 30 to 35 minutes.

*Oven Duxelles

Duxelles is minced mushrooms from which almost ⅔ of the moisture has been drawn out in a slow cooking process, resulting in an intensified flavor. It is an excellent seasoning for egg dishes and omelets, sauces, stuffings or dressings, fish, poultry and meat dishes, hors d'oeuvres, etc. Duxelles will keep in an airtight jar in the refrigerator several days and can be frozen indefinitely.

This oven method of preparing duxelles requires less effort than the usual method of sautéing the mushrooms in butter, and it is fat free. For added convenience, prepare several batches in 8-ounce quantities; 8 ounces of mushrooms (with stems) will weigh about 3½ ounces after baking. Select only firm mushrooms for baking. Once prepared they can be minced with a knife, in a food processor or in a blender in batches. Mushrooms can be stored either whole or minced.

Position rack in center of oven and preheat to 425°F. Wipe mushrooms clean with damp paper towel. Trim stem ends. Arrange mushrooms in single layer in baking dish. Bake 12 minutes. Reduce temperature to 375°F. Shake pan several times to loosen mushrooms. Continue baking, shaking pan occasionally, until mushrooms shrivel but are not hard, 20 to 50 minutes depending on size.

If duxelles is not used immediately, wrap in paper towels, place in plastic bag and chill for several hours. Remove toweling and refrigerate or freeze in airtight jar or plastic bag.

Buttermilk Chive Bread

Makes 2 loaves

Glaze
1 egg
½ teaspoon salt

Bread
1 envelope dry yeast
1 tablespoon sugar
½ cup plus 2 tablespoons warm water (105°F to 115°F)

2 cups (or more) bread flour
1 cup unbleached all purpose flour
1½ teaspoons salt
½ cup warm buttermilk (105°F to 115°F)
2 tablespoons minced fresh chives

Cornmeal

For glaze: Insert steel knife into processor and mix egg with salt 2 seconds; remove and set aside. Do not clean work bowl.

For bread: Oil large bowl and set aside. Combine yeast and sugar with warm water in small bowl and let stand until foamy, about 10 minutes.

Combine 2 cups bread flour, ½ cup all purpose flour and salt in processor work bowl. With machine running, add yeast mixture, buttermilk and chives through feed tube and mix 10 seconds. Continue mixing until dough comes away from sides of bowl, about 40 seconds, adding remaining all purpose flour 1 tablespoon at a time if dough is too wet (it should be sticky and elastic).

Transfer dough to oiled bowl, turning to coat all surfaces. Cover bowl with damp towel. Let stand in warm draft-free area (an oven preheated to lowest setting 2 minutes and then turned off works well; cushion bottom of bowl with pot holder) until dough has doubled in volume, about 1 hour.

Grease or oil double French bread pan or baking sheet and sprinkle with cornmeal. Transfer dough to well-floured surface. Work in additional flour until dough is easy to handle and no longer sticky. Divide dough in half. Roll half out into rectangle, then roll up lengthwise (as for jelly roll), pinching ends and seam tightly. Repeat with remaining dough. Transfer to pans (or baking sheet) seam side down. Cover lightly with damp towel and let stand in warm draft-free area until almost doubled in volume, about 45 minutes.

About 15 minutes before baking, position rack in center of oven and preheat to 425°F. Slash tops of loaves and brush with glaze, being careful not to drip glaze onto pan. Bake until loaves are deeply colored and sound hollow when tapped on bottom, about 25 to 30 minutes. Remove loaves from pans and let cool on wire rack.

Country Onion Bread

Thick slices of this crusty bread are perfect with winter soups and stews.

Makes 1 large or 2 small rounds

6 tablespoons (¾ stick) unsalted butter
1 tablespoon olive or vegetable oil
1 pound onions, finely diced
1½ teaspoons salt

1½ teaspoons caraway seeds
1½ teaspoons dill seeds
1¼ cups warm water

2 envelopes dry yeast
1 tablespoon firmly packed light brown sugar
½ cup warm water (105°F to 115°F)

¼ cup molasses
3 cups rye flour
3 cups (or more) unbleached all purpose flour

Cornmeal

Milk
½ teaspoon caraway seeds
½ teaspoon dill seeds

Melt butter with oil in heavy large skillet over medium-low heat. Add onions and cook until softened and translucent, stirring occasionally, about 10 minutes. Stir in salt. Cool.

Stir 1½ teaspoons each caraway seeds and dill seeds into 1¼ cups warm water. Let stand 20 minutes.

Sprinkle yeast and sugar into ½ cup warm water in bowl of heavy-duty mixer fitted with dough hook; stir to dissolve. Let mixture stand until foamy and proofed, about 5 minutes.

Add water-seed mixture and molasses to yeast mixture. Add 1 cup each rye and all purpose flour and mix until dough is smooth, about 1 minute. Add remaining flour ½ cup at a time, alternating with onion mixture (including butter and oil in skillet) and knead until dough is smooth, elastic and cleans sides of bowl, 8 to 10 minutes. (Dough can also be made by hand.)

Oil large bowl. Add dough, turning to coat entire surface. Cover with plastic wrap and kitchen towel and let rise in warm draft-free area until doubled in volume, about 1 hour.

Line baking sheet with parchment paper; sprinkle with cornmeal. Punch dough down. Turn out onto well-floured surface and knead gently 3 to 4 minutes (dough should be springy).

Knead dough into smooth 3-inch-high round. (Or, divide in half and knead each half into smooth 3-inch-high round.) Transfer to prepared sheet. Cover dough with dampened towel and let rise in warm draft-free area until almost doubled in volume, approximately 35 minutes.

Position rack in center of oven and preheat to 375°F. Make 3 parallel ¼-inch-deep slashes in tops of rounds. Brush lightly with milk. Sprinkle with ½ teaspoon each caraway seeds and dill seeds. Bake until rounds are rich brown and sound hollow when tapped on bottom, about 40 minutes. (If tops brown too quickly, cover with parchment.) Cool bread 2 hours on rack before slicing. (*Can be prepared 1 day ahead. Wrap in plastic and store at room temperature. Reheat unwrapped bread 5 to 7 minutes in 350°F oven.*)

Onion Braid

This combination of ingredients results in a batter that has more substance than most, providing the firmness needed to weave it easily into a braid.

Makes 1 large loaf

1 envelope dry yeast
¼ cup warm water (105°F to 115°F)
4 cups bread flour
1 cup nonfat milk, heated to between 100°F and 110°F
¼ cup (½ stick) unsalted butter, room temperature
¼ cup sugar
1 extra-large egg or 2 medium eggs
1½ teaspoons salt

Filling
¼ cup (½ stick) unsalted butter
3 large onions, minced

3 tablespoons freshly grated Parmesan cheese
2 tablespoons chopped fresh parsley
2 tablespoons toasted sesame seeds
½ teaspoon garlic salt
½ teaspoon paprika

Glaze
1 egg yolk
1 teaspoon water
Sesame seeds

Sprinkle yeast over water in large bowl of electric mixer and let proof about 5 minutes. Add 2 cups flour, milk, ¼ cup butter, sugar, egg(s) and salt and blend at medium speed until combined. Add remaining flour and mix until soft dough forms. Cover and let rise in warm area until doubled, about 1 hour.

While dough is rising, prepare filling. Melt butter in large skillet over medium heat. Add onion and sauté until soft and pale golden. Remove from heat and add remaining ingredients for filling. Mix well, then set aside to cool.

When dough has doubled, stir it down and transfer to floured work surface. Roll or pat into 18 × 12-inch rectangle.

Spread filling evenly over surface. Cut dough into three 4 × 18-inch strips. Roll each strip into a rope, sealing edges and ends well. Braid ropes loosely and transfer to greased baking sheet. Cover and let rise in warm area for 1 hour.

Preheat oven to 350°F. Combine egg yolk with water and brush over top for glaze. Sprinkle with sesame seeds. Bake until loaf is golden brown, about 30 to 35 minutes. Transfer to rack and let cool before slicing.

Herb and Onion Bread Braids

Makes 2 small loaves

1 tablespoon butter
1/2 medium onion, chopped (about 1/2 cup)
1 garlic clove, minced
2 tablespoons minced fresh parsley
1/2 teaspoon dried marjoram
1/4 teaspoon dried sage
1/4 teaspoon dried thyme

1/2 cup warm water (105°F to 115°F)
1 1/2 teaspoons dry yeast

1/2 teaspoon salt
1/2 teaspoon sugar
2 to 2 1/2 cups bread flour
2 tablespoons (1/4 stick) butter, room temperature

1 egg, beaten
Coarse salt (optional)

Oil large bowl and set aside. Melt 1 tablespoon butter in medium skillet over low heat. Add onion, garlic and herbs and cook until onion is translucent, about 5 minutes. Let cool.

Combine water, yeast, salt and sugar in another large bowl. Let stand until foamy, about 5 minutes. Add 1 cup flour, onion mixture and 2 tablespoons butter and beat well. Add enough remaining flour to form soft dough. Turn out onto lightly floured surface and knead about 5 minutes. Transfer to prepared bowl, turning to coat all surfaces. Cover bowl and let dough stand in warm draft-free area until doubled in volume, about 1 1/2 hours.

Lightly grease baking sheet and set aside. Punch dough down, turn out onto work surface and knead lightly. Divide dough into 6 equal portions. Shape each into strand about 3/4 inch in diameter and 8 to 9 inches long. Pinch 3 strands together at one end, sprinkling with water if necessary to make strands adhere. Braid dough strands, pinching other ends together firmly. Repeat with remaining 3 strands to make 2 loaves.

Transfer loaves to prepared baking sheet. Cover with towel. Let stand in warm draft-free area until doubled in volume, about 45 minutes to 1 hour.

Preheat oven to 425°F. Brush loaves with egg and sprinkle with coarse salt if desired. Bake until loaves are golden brown and sound hollow when tapped, 20 to 30 minutes. Cool on racks.

Garlic Focaccia (Focaccia all'Aglio)

An easy, no-knead bread.

Makes 1 loaf

Sponge

1 cup plus 1 tablespoon
   unbleached all purpose flour
2 envelopes dry yeast
½ cup warm water (105°F to 115°F)

¼ cup olive oil
10 large garlic cloves, unpeeled
½ cup dry white wine

Batter

2 cups unbleached all purpose flour
Pinch of salt
Freshly ground pepper
1 cup warm milk (105°F to 115°F)

Olive oil (for pan)

For sponge: Place 1 cup flour in large bowl and make well in center. Sprinkle yeast over ½ cup warm water in small bowl; stir to dissolve. Pour into well. Using wooden spoon, gradually draw flour from inner edge of well into center until half of flour is incorporated. Sprinkle remaining 1 tablespoon flour over top. Cover bowl with towel. Let sponge rise in warm draft-free area until doubled, about 1 hour.

Meanwhile, heat olive oil in heavy small saucepan over medium heat. Add garlic and sauté 5 minutes. Transfer 5 garlic cloves to plate and set aside for garnish. Add wine to remaining garlic. Reduce heat and simmer until all but 1 tablespoon liquid is absorbed and garlic is soft. Transfer garlic to work surface, using slotted spoon. Discard skins and mash garlic with fork. Mix with cooking juices to form paste.

For batter: Place remaining 2 cups flour in another large bowl. Make well in center. Transfer sponge and flour in bottom of bowl to well. Blend garlic paste, salt and pepper into sponge. Gradually stir in milk while drawing flour from inner edge of well into center. Stir until all flour is incorporated. Cover and let rise in warm draft-free area until doubled, about 45 minutes.

Preheat oven to 400°F. Coat 8¾ × 13½-inch baking dish generously with olive oil. Pour in batter, smoothing with rubber spatula. Peel reserved garlic and arrange over top. Bake until bread is golden brown, about 35 minutes. Cool on rack 15 minutes before serving.

French Pepper-Crackling Bread

Makes 2 loaves

1 pound pork fat from loin or
  1 pound very fatty, thick-cut
  bacon, cut into ½-inch pieces
½ cup minced shallots
1 teaspoon minced garlic

1 tablespoon dry yeast
1 teaspoon sugar
½ cup warm water (105°F to 115°F)

3 eggs, room temperature
1 egg yolk, room temperature

1 cup warm water (105°F to 115°F)
5 to 5½ cups all purpose flour
1 teaspoon salt
1 teaspoon freshly cracked pepper
6 tablespoons (¾ stick) unsalted
  butter, room temperature

1 egg beaten with 1 tablespoon
  milk (glaze)

Cook pork fat in heavy medium skillet over low heat until crisp and golden, stirring frequently, about 45 minutes. Remove with slotted spoon and drain on paper towels. Chop cracklings coarsely and set aside. Drain all but 2 tablespoons fat from skillet. Add shallots and stir until lightly colored, about 5 minutes. Blend in garlic. Cool to room temperature.

Stir yeast and 1 teaspoon sugar into ½ cup warm water in large bowl. Cover mixture with towel and let stand until foamy, about 5 minutes.

Mix eggs and yolk into yeast until smooth. Stir in 1 cup warm water, then 1½ cups flour, shallot mixture, salt and pepper. Blend in remaining flour, 1 cup at a time, alternately with butter, adding enough flour to form soft, slightly sticky dough. Turn dough out onto lightly floured surface and knead in cracklings ½ cup at a time. Continue kneading dough until smooth and elastic, about 6 minutes, kneading in additional flour as necessary. Butter large bowl. Add dough, turning to coat entire surface. Cover with plastic wrap and towel. Let dough rise until doubled in volume, about 1 hour.

Punch dough down. Turn out onto lightly floured surface and knead until smooth, 2 minutes. Divide dough in half. Cover and let rest 10 minutes.

Line 2 baking sheets with parchment paper. Form each half of dough into 8 × 5-inch oval. Transfer to prepared sheets. Cover each with kitchen towel. Let rise at room temperature until almost doubled, about 1 hour.

Position rack in center of oven and preheat to 375°F. Brush loaves with egg glaze. Slash top of each loaf ⅛ inch deep in decorative pattern, using sharp knife dipped in flour. Bake until loaves are golden and sound hollow when tapped on bottoms, about 40 minutes. Cool completely on racks. *(Can be wrapped and stored at room temperature 3 days or frozen up to 1 month. Reheat thawed unwrapped bread in 350°F oven for about 5 minutes.)*

Burgundian Walnut Bread

Makes 2 loaves

½ cup (1 stick) butter or walnut oil
1½ cups finely chopped onion

2 cups warm milk (105°F to 115°F)
2 envelopes dry yeast
2 tablespoons sugar

5 to 6 cups all purpose flour
2 tablespoons salt

½ cup coarsely chopped toasted walnuts

Melt butter (or heat oil) in medium saucepan over medium heat. Add onion and cook until transparent. Cool.

Grease large mixing bowl and two 1-quart round baking dishes. Set aside. Combine milk, yeast and sugar in medium bowl and let stand until foamy and proofed, about 5 minutes. Add 5 cups flour to yeast mixture with salt and mix well. Turn dough out onto lightly floured surface and knead until smooth and elastic, about 5 to 10 minutes, adding remaining flour as necessary until dough is no longer sticky. Transfer dough to prepared bowl, cover with towel and let rise in warm draft-free area until doubled in volume, about 2 hours.

Punch dough down. Turn out onto floured surface. Knead, adding onion and walnuts, until dough is smooth, satiny and firm, about 3 minutes, adding small amounts of flour if necessary. Shape into 2 round loaves and turn into prepared baking dishes. Cover with towel and let rise until almost doubled, about 30 to 40 minutes.

Preheat oven to 400°F. Bake loaves until browned, about 45 minutes. Turn out onto wire racks to cool.

Gwyn's Herb Pinwheel Rolls

Makes 16

1 envelope dry yeast
¼ cup warm water (105°F to 115°F)
1 cup milk, scalded with
   1 tablespoon butter and cooled
   to lukewarm
1 tablespoon sugar
1 teaspoon salt
3½ cups (about) bread flour

1 medium onion, chopped and
   sautéed in butter until tender but
   not browned
2 teaspoons dried dillweed
   Melted butter

Generously grease large bowl and 10-inch round baking pan. Sprinkle yeast over warm water in large bowl and let stand until foamy and proofed, about 10 minutes. Stir in milk, sugar and salt. Add 2 cups flour and beat well. Add 1 more cup flour and mix thoroughly.

Turn dough out onto lightly floured surface and knead in remaining flour until dough is smooth and satiny, about 10 minutes. Place in greased bowl, turning to coat entire surface. Cover and let rise in warm area until doubled, 1½ hours.

Punch dough down and knead several times. Roll into 16 × 11-inch rectangle. Sprinkle evenly with onion, then with dillweed. Roll lengthwise jelly roll fashion. Slice into 1-inch pieces and arrange in prepared 10-inch pan so rolls barely touch. Brush with butter and let rise until doubled, 30 to 45 minutes.

Preheat oven to 375°F. Bake rolls until golden brown, about 30 minutes. Serve warm.

Rosemary-Savory Rolls

Makes 20

1 cup water
⅓ cup butter or lard, melted and
   cooled slightly

1 teaspoon dried savory
¾ teaspoon dried rosemary

3½ to 4 cups unbleached all purpose
   flour
¼ to ⅓ cup sugar
1 tablespoon dry yeast

1 teaspoon salt
1 egg, well beaten

6 tablespoons (¾ stick) butter,
   melted

1 egg white, beaten with
   1 tablespoon cold water (glaze)

Bring water to boil. Remove from heat and stir in ⅓ cup melted butter. Let mixture cool to 130°F to 135°F.

Crush savory and rosemary in mortar with pestle. Set herbs aside.

Combine 1 cup flour, sugar to taste, yeast and salt in large bowl of heavy-duty mixer. Add water mixture and beat until slowly dissolving ribbon forms when beaters are lifted, about 2 minutes. Add ½ cup flour, egg and herbs and beat until batter thickens, about 1 minute. Beat in 2 cups flour 1 cup at a time. Cover bowl with towel. Let dough stand for 10 minutes.

Turn dough out onto lightly floured surface. Wipe bowl clean; grease well. Knead dough until smooth and elastic, adding up to ½ cup more flour if necessary to prevent sticking, about 10 minutes. Add dough to bowl, turning to coat entire surface. Cover with plastic wrap and refrigerate 2 hours. (*Can be prepared 4 days ahead and refrigerated.*)

Brush 20 muffin cups generously with some of melted butter. Cut dough into 20 pieces. Roll each piece into round. Dip rounds in remaining melted butter.

Place in muffin cups. Let stand in warm draft-free area until doubled in volume, 1 to 1½ hours.

Position rack in center of oven and preheat to 400°F. Brush rolls with glaze. Bake until golden brown, about 12 minutes (if rolls brown too quickly, cover with foil). Serve immediately.

Beijing Flower Rolls

These yeast rolls resemble a flower bud just opening. Steaming gives them a soft, delicate texture—a wonderful contrast to roasted meats and poultry.

Makes about 15

1 recipe Yeast Dough*
1 tablespoon oriental sesame oil

Filling (optional)
¾ cup chopped green onion

¾ cup minced well-flavored smoked ham

All purpose flour

Divide dough in half. Return half to bowl and cover with towel. Roll remainder into rectangle about 8 × 12 inches and ⅙ inch thick. Brush surface with half of sesame oil. If using filling, sprinkle green onion and ham evenly over top but leave 1-inch border on side closest to you. Roll dough lengthwise jelly roll fashion to make log about 1 inch in diameter. Repeat with remaining dough. Cut both cylinders of dough into 1-inch pieces.

To form rolls, stack 2 pieces of dough smooth side together on work surface (cut edges will show on sides) and press firmly. Repeat until all pieces are used.

Dip dull edge of knife blade into flour. Press blade firmly crosswise into center of each roll (this causes edges to rise and form flower shape). Set roll on lightly floured tray and cover with dry towel. Repeat with remaining pieces. Let rise in warm draft-free area until doubled, about 30 to 40 minutes.

Bring about 1½ inches of water to boil in wok. Line steamer plate with damp cloth. Set rolls on cloth, making sure they do not touch. Set over water, cover and steam about 15 minutes over medium-high heat. Turn off heat and wait until steam subsides, about 2 minutes. If necessary, transfer rolls to large cloth to dry excess moisture. Transfer to platter and serve.

Flower rolls can be steamed several hours ahead. Leave at room temperature and resteam 10 minutes just before serving.

Steamed rolls can be refrigerated up to 10 days or frozen up to 4 weeks. Cool completely, then wrap in plastic and overwrap with plastic bag or foil. To reheat, remove from refrigerator or freezer, discard wrapping and resteam 15 minutes.

Variation

After rolls are steamed, fry a few at a time in oil heated to 350°F until rolls are golden brown on both sides. Drain and serve immediately.

*Yeast Dough

A deliciously flavored, fine-textured dough, perfect for steamed and baked baos (buns) and steamed Chinese bread. The combination of flours and two leavening agents are responsible for the superb character of this dough.

2 tablespoons warm water (105°F to 115°F)
½ teaspoon dry yeast
1 tablespoon sugar

½ cup milk
1 tablespoon salted butter

1¼ cups bread flour or gluten flour (hard wheat flour)

½ cup cake flour (soft wheat flour)
¼ teaspoon salt
Additional hard wheat flour (for kneading)
¼ teaspoon peanut oil

½ teaspoon baking powder

Combine water, sugar and yeast and let stand until foamy and proofed, about 15 minutes.

Combine milk and butter in saucepan and heat to between 100°F and 115°F, stirring to melt butter.

Combine flours and salt in bowl. Add yeast. Slowly pour in warm milk and stir in one direction until thoroughly blended. Turn dough out onto lightly floured work surface and knead until smooth and elastic, about 5 to 10 minutes, adding flour as necessary until dough is no longer sticky. (To test whether dough has been sufficiently kneaded, make indentation with fingers; if dough springs back, it is ready for rising.) Rub oil onto surface of dough and place in large bowl. Cover and let rise in warm draft-free area until doubled, about 3 hours.

Punch dough down with fist. Turn onto floured work surface and roll into rectangle about 9 × 12 inches. Sprinkle with baking powder. Fold dough over and knead until smooth, satiny and firm, about 3 minutes, adding small amount of flour if necessary. The dough is now ready to be shaped.

5 ❦ Sweet Yeast Breads and Rolls

Sweet yeast breads are festive in a way that few other foods can match; holiday breads alone could fill a fair-size cookbook. The assortment here comprises traditional breads from all the corners of Europe as well as new recipes that you will want to establish as traditions of your own.

For old-fashioned appeal try Babci's Bread, Ukrainian Sweet Bread or Sally Lunn (pages 48 and 49). Each is rich and buttery, but simple enough to serve as a superb foil for homemade spreads and preserves. There are also several cinnamon rolls, sticky buns and raised Pumpkin Biscuits (pages 69 to 72) to accompany hearty country-style breakfast and brunch fare.

As for special-occasion sweet breads, you will find a plenitude of choices here. Nearly every European country is represented and there are two Mexican versions as well—including a whimsical Alligator Bread (page 51) that makes a spectacular buffet centerpiece. This recipe, like the Swiss bread dolls known as *Grittibanz* (page 58), will let you be as artistic as you please—and you just may want to bring the whole family in on the fun.

Babci's Bread

Makes four 9 × 5-inch loaves and one 7 × 3-inch loaf

4 cups milk
1/3 cup warm water (105°F to 115°F)
2 tablespoons sugar
3 yeast cakes
6 cups sifted unbleached all purpose flour

6 eggs
1¼ cups sugar
10 tablespoons (1¼ sticks) butter

3 tablespoons solid vegetable shortening
1 tablespoon salt
½ teaspoon finely grated lemon peel
10 cups sifted unbleached all purpose flour

1 teaspoon water

Grease four 9 × 5-inch glass loaf pans and one 7 × 3-inch glass loaf pan. Grease large bowl and set aside. Scald milk. Transfer to large bowl and cool to 105°F to 115°F. Combine water and sugar in small bowl. Add yeast cakes and mash until dissolved. Add to cooled milk. Stir in 6 cups flour and beat until smooth using wooden spoon. Cover bowl with dry cloth and let dough rise in warm draft-free area until doubled in volume, about 2 hours.

Beat eggs in large bowl to blend. Measure 2 tablespoons egg and set aside. Mix sugar into remaining eggs. Melt butter and shortening in small saucepan over medium-low heat. Stir in salt and lemon peel. Add butter mixture and egg mixture to dough and stir well. Add 9 cups flour and mix well. Sprinkle work surface with some of remaining 1 cup flour. Knead dough on prepared surface about 15 minutes, dusting with remaining flour as necessary. Transfer dough to greased bowl, turning to coat entire surface. Cover with damp cloth and let rise in warm draft-free area until doubled in volume, about 2 hours. Punch dough down. Let rise until doubled, about 1 hour.

Preheat oven to 375°F. Punch dough down and transfer to lightly floured surface. Divide into 5 parts, 1 slightly smaller than remaining 4. Pat each piece into oval. Roll dough pieces up loosely, as for jelly roll, and arrange seam side down in prepared pans. Cover each loaf with dry cloth and let rise in warm draft-free area 15 to 20 minutes. Combine reserved egg and 1 teaspoon water in small bowl. Brush top of each loaf with mixture. Bake 10 minutes. Reduce oven temperature to 350°F and continue baking until loaves sound hollow when tapped on bottom, about 30 to 35 minutes. Cool 10 minutes in pans. Remove loaves from pans and transfer to rack. Cool completely before slicing.

Ukrainian Sweet Bread

Makes three 8½ × 4½-inch loaves

1 cup (2 sticks) butter, room temperature
½ cup sugar
1 teaspoon salt
3 eggs, room temperature
2 cups milk

1 envelope dry yeast
8 cups all purpose flour

1 egg, room temperature, beaten to blend

Grease three 8½ × 4½-inch loaf pans. Combine butter, sugar and salt in large bowl and mix well. Add eggs one at a time, beating well after each addition. Bring milk to boil in small saucepan over medium-high heat. Skim top; let milk stand until cooled to 95°F to 115°F. Combine yeast and about ½ cup cooled milk in small bowl and stir until yeast dissolves. Add remaining milk and yeast mixture alternately to butter mixture with flour, blending slowly and stirring well after each addition. Transfer dough to lightly floured surface and knead 3 to 4 minutes.

Return dough to bowl. Cover with towel and let rise in warm draft-free area until doubled in volume, about 2 hours.

Punch dough down. Transfer to lightly floured surface and knead 3 to 4 minutes. Return dough to bowl. Cover with towel and let rise in warm draft-free area until increased by 1/4, about 45 minutes.

Punch dough down and divide into 3 pieces. Shape each into loaf. Transfer to prepared pans. Cover loaves with towels and let rise in warm draft-free area until dough rises to tops of pans, about 30 more minutes.

Preheat oven to 325°F. Brush top of each loaf with beaten egg. Bake until bread is dark golden in color, about 60 minutes. Cool loaves in pans for 10 minutes before turning out and serving.

Sally Lunn Bread with Flavored Butters

6 to 8 servings

1 cup milk
1/2 cup (1 stick) butter, room temperature
1/4 cup water

1/2 cup honey
3 eggs, beaten to blend
2 teaspoons salt

1 teaspoon vanilla
1/2 teaspoon almond extract
3 1/2 cups unbleached all purpose flour
2 envelopes dry yeast

Honey-Lemon Butter*
Strawberry Butter**

Heat milk in heavy medium saucepan. Remove from heat. Add butter and water and stir until butter melts. Cool to lukewarm.

Transfer mixture to large bowl of electric mixer. Stir in honey, eggs, salt, vanilla and almond extract. Add flour and yeast and beat until well blended. Cover with towel and let rise in warm draft-free area until doubled in volume, 45 to 60 minutes.

Preheat oven to 350°F. Grease 9-inch tube pan. Punch dough down. Fit into prepared pan. Bake until tester inserted in center comes out clean, about 50 minutes. Serve bread warm with honey-lemon butter and strawberry butter.

*Honey-Lemon Butter

Makes 1 cup

1/2 cup (1 stick) butter, room temperature
1/4 cup honey

2 tablespoons fresh lemon juice
1 tablespoon finely grated lemon peel

Blend all ingredients in small bowl until smooth. Cover and refrigerate. Bring to room temperature before serving.

**Strawberry Butter

Makes 1 cup

1/4 cup (1/2 stick) butter, room temperature
1 1/4 cups powdered sugar

1/4 cup crushed fresh strawberries
1/2 teaspoon vanilla
Pinch of salt

Cream butter with sugar in medium bowl. Blend in strawberries, vanilla and salt. Cover and refrigerate at least 2 hours. Bring to room temperature before serving.

American Chocolate Bread

Chocolate-filled loaves are a special treat for breakfast or tea.

Makes 8 small loaves

Sponge
1½ cups unbleached all purpose flour or bread flour
 1 cup warm water (105°F to 115°F)
 2 envelopes dry yeast
 2 tablespoons honey

Dough
 1 cup lukewarm milk (95°F)

 3 tablespoons butter, melted
 1 tablespoon salt

4 to 5 cups unbleached all purpose flour or bread flour

8 ounces semisweet chocolate, coarsely chopped

1 egg beaten with 2 tablespoons whipping cream (glaze)
 Sugar

For sponge: Whisk flour, water, yeast and honey in large bowl until smooth. Cover with plastic. Let stand in warm draft-free area 1 hour.

For dough: Stir down sponge, using wooden spoon. Blend in milk, butter and salt. Mix in enough flour ½ cup at a time to form soft dough. Knead on floured surface until smooth and no longer sticky, adding more flour if necessary, about 10 minutes.

Grease large bowl. Add dough, turning to coat entire surface. Cover bowl with plastic. Let rise in warm draft-free area until doubled, about 1¼ hours.

Grease eight 2½ × 4½-inch loaf pans. Gently knead dough on lightly floured surface until deflated. Pat out to ¾-inch-thick rectangle. Cut into 8 even pieces. Pat each out into 4 × 7-inch rectangle. Spread 1 ounce chocolate on short end of each. Roll up jelly roll fashion. Pinch seam and ends to seal. Arrange seam side down in prepared pans. Cover with kitchen towel. Let rise for 15 minutes to lighten.

Preheat oven to 375°F. Brush loaves with egg glaze and sprinkle with sugar. Bake until light brown and loaves sound hollow when tapped on bottom, about 30 minutes. Immediately remove from pans. Cool on racks 10 minutes. Serve loaves hot.

For variation, spread 1 tablespoon raspberry preserves on short end of dough before adding chopped chocolate.

French Brioche Wreath

Makes 1 large wreath

1⅓ cups milk
 10 tablespoons (1¼ sticks) unsalted butter
 ¼ cup sugar
 1 envelope dry yeast

 2 eggs
 1 egg yolk
1¼ teaspoons salt

1 teaspoon almond extract

6 cups (about) unbleached all purpose flour

⅓ cup finely diced blanched almonds, lightly toasted

1 egg yolk beaten with 2 tablespoons water (glaze)

Heat milk with butter in heavy small saucepan over low heat until butter melts. Stir in sugar until dissolved. Pour into large bowl of heavy-duty electric mixer and let stand until warm (105°F to 115°F). Stir yeast into milk mixture. Cover with towel and let stand until foamy, about 8 minutes.

Beat eggs and egg yolk into milk mixture one at a time using dough hook. Blend in salt and extract. Mix in flour 1 cup at a time until dough gathers on hook and is slightly sticky. Stir in nuts. Knead dough until smooth and very elastic, at least 10 minutes.

Generously butter bowl. Add dough, turning to coat entire surface. Cover bowl with plastic wrap and towel. Let rise in warm draft-free area until doubled in volume, about 2 hours.

Punch dough down. Turn out onto lightly floured surface and knead 4 minutes. Wash, dry and rebutter bowl. Return dough to bowl, turning to coat entire surface. Cover and let rise again until doubled, about 1 hour.

Punch dough down. Turn out onto lightly floured surface and knead 3 minutes. Cover; let rest 10 minutes.

Line baking sheet with parchment paper. Shape dough into 9-inch round. Transfer to baking sheet and pat down gently to 2 inches high. Press hole into center of loaf with lightly floured fingers. Gently pull against inner sides of dough to widen opening to 5-inch diameter. Cover loaf with kitchen towel. Let rise at room temperature until almost doubled, about 1 hour.

Preheat oven to 375°F. Brush loaf with egg glaze. Texture wreath by snipping entire upper surface with sharp scissors dipped in water. Bake until loaf is golden brown and sounds hollow when tapped on bottom, about 30 minutes. Cool on rack. *(Can be wrapped and stored at room temperature 2 days or frozen up to 1 month.)*

Cooled loaf can be iced before wrapping or serving. Sift ½ cup powdered sugar; mix with ½ teaspoon almond extract and 1 to 2 tablespoons milk to spreadable consistency. Garnish loaf with glacéed fruits and whole almonds.

Mexican Alligator Bread

The recipe for this whimsical bread was inspired by Francisco Valle of La Mexicana Bakery in San Francisco.

Makes 2 loaves

¼ cup warm milk (105°F to 115°F)
1 envelope dry yeast*
½ cup sugar

6 tablespoons (¾ stick) unsalted butter
4 eggs, room temperature
Grated peel of 1 large lemon
½ teaspoon salt
4 cups all purpose flour

4 raisins
1 egg, beaten to blend

2 maraschino cherries

Royal Icing
2 teaspoons egg white
10 to 12 tablespoons powdered sugar

Butter large mixing bowl and grease 2 baking sheets; set aside. Combine milk, yeast and 1 teaspoon sugar in small bowl and stir until yeast is dissolved. Let stand until foamy and proofed, about 10 minutes.

Combine butter and remaining sugar in large bowl of electric mixer and beat at medium speed until creamy. Add eggs, lemon peel, salt and yeast mixture and mix well. Beat in flour 1 cup at a time until well blended. Continue beating at high speed about 5 minutes.

Turn dough out onto lightly floured surface and knead until smooth, about 5 to 7 minutes. Shape into ball. Transfer to buttered bowl, turning to coat entire surface. Cover with towel and let rise in warm draft-free area (85°F) until doubled in volume, about 1½ hours. Punch dough down and let rise again until doubled, about 1¼ hours. Punch down again and divide in half. Shape each half into ball; let stand at room temperature 5 minutes.

To form alligator, slap 1 ball of dough onto lightly floured surface. Pat into 4 × 9-inch rectangle. Roll dough up lengthwise, pinching ends and seam well.

Slap seam side down onto surface, then roll evenly with palms of hands into cylinder 16 inches long. Transfer to prepared baking sheet. Cut 1-inch slit horizontally through center of one end of roll. Using fingers and knife, open slit to shape mouth. Cut 2½ × 4½-inch rectangle of heavy cardboard. Cover completely with foil and grease well. Fold in half crosswise and insert in mouth to hold shape during rising and baking. Shape dough around cardboard, pressing until it adheres (sprinkle with water if necessary).

To form front legs, make 4-inch tapered cut beginning 1 inch behind mouth and ½ inch in from right side of body. Repeat on left side. Pull front legs away from body. To form back legs, make 4-inch tapered cut, beginning 4 inches from tail end and ½ inch in from right side of body. Repeat on left side. Pull back legs away from body. Shape tail and curve body slightly. Press 2 raisins firmly behind mouth into head for eyes. Brush alligator with beaten egg. Let stand 5 minutes and brush again. Repeat with remaining dough. *(Can be made ahead to this point and refrigerated overnight.)* Let rise in warm draft-free area until doubled in volume, about 1½ hours (allow extra time if dough has been refrigerated). Press dough back against cardboard if mouths begin to loosen.

Preheat oven to 350°F. Using scissors, cut 3 rows of scales by snipping and pulling up dough into a point down backs of alligators. (Center row should extend down tail.) Bake alligators until nicely browned, about 20 to 25 minutes. Transfer to rack to cool. Gently remove cardboard from mouths and press cherries into back of throats.

For icing: Place egg white in small bowl. Add sugar 1 tablespoon at a time, stirring with fork until icing is stiff enough to stand in peaks. If not using immediately, cover with damp paper towel to prevent drying.

Fill pastry bag with icing and pipe jagged teeth into upper and lower jaws.

*If time permits, use only half of yeast, allowing bread to rise slowly and develop maximum flavor.

Springtime Bread

Makes 1 loaf (24 rolls)

½ cup milk
½ cup water
½ cup honey
¼ cup (½ stick) butter
2 tablespoons rum or fresh orange juice

½ cup warm water (105°F to 115°F)
2 tablespoons dry yeast
1 teaspoon honey

3 eggs, beaten
1 teaspoon fresh lemon juice
1 teaspoon salt
½ teaspoon cinnamon
½ teaspoon finely grated orange peel
½ teaspoon ground coriander
7 cups unbleached all purpose flour

Fresh orange juice

Oil large bowl. Line baking sheet or 12-inch pizza pan with aluminum foil, bringing foil up 2 inches around sides to form collar. Grease bottom of foil.

Bring milk and water to boil in small saucepan over high heat. Remove from heat and add ½ cup honey, butter and rum or orange juice. Stir until butter is melted; cool to room temperature.

Combine warm water, yeast and 1 teaspoon honey in large mixing bowl and stir until yeast is dissolved. Let stand until foamy, about 5 minutes.

Add milk mixture, eggs, lemon juice, salt, cinnamon, orange peel and coriander. Stir in 3½ cups flour. Beat in one direction for 100 strokes. Let stand until mixture bubbles, about 20 minutes. Beat in remaining flour.

Turn dough out onto lightly floured surface and knead until soft, about 7 minutes. Transfer to oiled bowl, turning to coat all surfaces. Cover and let rise in warm draft-free area until doubled in bulk, about 1 hour.

Punch dough down and knead several times to rid dough of any air bubbles. Divide dough into 24 pieces, reserving small portion for decoration. Shape pieces into rolls. Arrange in prepared pan with sides touching. Roll out reserved dough; cut out small birds and fish with sharp knife. Arrange on top of rolls. Brush each roll with orange juice. Cover and let rise until doubled.

Preheat oven to 350°F. Bake until golden brown, about 50 minutes. Let cool 5 minutes. Turn loaf out onto rack and let cool completely.

Italian Buccellati

A sweet, wine-scented bread ring that is a specialty of the town of Lucca in Tuscany. Wrap "candy cane" fashion with shiny red, white and green ribbons and present with a bottle of Marsala or other Italian wine. Good with cheeses such as Bel Paese or Fontina.

Makes three 8-inch rings

1 cup milk	2/3 cup sugar
2 teaspoons whole aniseed	2 eggs
2 teaspoons grated lemon peel	2 egg yolks
1 envelope dry yeast	5 to 6 cups all purpose flour
1/2 teaspoon sugar	1/2 teaspoon salt
1/4 cup warm water (105°F to 115°F)	1/4 cup Marsala
1/2 cup (1 stick) unsalted butter, room temperature	1 egg white, beaten to blend (glaze)

Scald milk with aniseed and lemon peel in heavy small saucepan. Cool to lukewarm. Stir yeast and 1/2 teaspoon sugar into 1/4 cup warm water in small bowl. Cover with towel and let stand until foamy, about 5 minutes.

Cream butter with sugar in large bowl until light and creamy. Mix in eggs and egg yolks one at a time until smooth. Mix in yeast. Stir in 1 cup flour with salt. Add Marsala with milk mixture. Blend in remaining flour 1 cup at a time until slightly sticky dough forms.

Turn dough out onto lightly floured surface and knead until smooth and elastic, about 6 minutes. Butter large bowl. Add dough, turning to coat entire surface. Cover with plastic wrap and towel. Let dough rise in warm area until doubled, about 1 hour.

Punch dough down. Turn out onto lightly floured surface and knead 2 minutes. Cover; let rest 10 minutes.

Line 3 baking sheets with parchment paper. Divide dough into 3 pieces. Shape each into flattened 5-inch round. Transfer to prepared sheets. Press hole in center of each round with lightly floured fingers. Gently pull against inner sides of dough to widen opening to 3-inch diameter (overall diameter of loaf should be 8 inches). Cover each loaf with towel. Let rise at room temperature until almost doubled in volume, about 30 minutes.

Position rack in center of oven and preheat to 375°F. Brush egg glaze over each ring. Bake until loaves are golden brown and sound hollow when tapped on bottom, about 25 minutes. Cool on racks. *(Can be wrapped and stored at room temperature 3 days or frozen up to 1 month. Reheat thawed unwrapped loaf in 350°F oven for 5 minutes.)*

Czechoslovakian Vanocka

A handsome braided bread perfect with coffee or hot mulled wine.

Makes 1 large loaf

1 cup milk
½ cup (1 stick) unsalted butter
⅓ cup honey
1 teaspoon salt
2 envelopes dry yeast
1 teaspoon firmly packed light brown sugar
½ cup warm water (105°F to 115°F)
½ cup golden raisins
½ cup slivered almonds, lightly toasted
2 tablespoons all purpose flour
⅓ cup firmly packed light brown sugar

3 egg yolks, room temperature
1 tablespoon grated lemon peel
1 teaspoon crushed aniseed
5 to 6 cups unbleached all purpose flour

Milk

1 egg yolk beaten with 1½ tablespoons whipping cream (glaze)
⅓ cup slivered almonds
3 tablespoons sugar

Heat milk with butter and honey in heavy small saucepan over low heat until butter melts. Stir in salt. Cool to lukewarm. Meanwhile, stir yeast and 1 teaspoon brown sugar into ½ cup warm water in large bowl. Cover with towel and let stand until foamy, about 5 minutes. Toss raisins and ½ cup almonds with 2 tablespoons flour.

Add milk mixture, ⅓ cup brown sugar, yolks, lemon peel and aniseed to yeast. Stir in 1 cup flour and raisin-nut mixture. Blend in remaining flour 1 cup at a time until soft, slightly sticky dough forms. Turn out onto lightly floured surface and knead until smooth and elastic, about 6 minutes, kneading in additional flour as necessary. Butter large bowl. Add dough, turning to coat entire surface. Cover with plastic wrap and towel. Let dough rise in warm draft-free area until doubled in volume, about 1½ hours.

Line large baking sheet with parchment paper. Punch dough down. Turn out onto lightly floured surface. Knead until smooth, 1 to 2 minutes. Divide into 5 equal pieces. Cover and let rest 10 minutes. Roll each piece into 12-inch-long rope. Place 3 ropes on prepared sheet and braid together. Pinch loose ends together and tuck under loaf. Twist remaining 2 ropes together. Brush top of 3-rope braid with milk. Place twisted ropes atop braid, pinch ends together, then tuck under. Cover with towel. Let rise until almost doubled, about 45 minutes.

Preheat oven to 350°F. Bake bread 35 minutes. Brush with egg glaze and sprinkle with ⅓ cup almonds. Continue baking until bread is golden brown and sounds hollow when tapped on bottom, about 20 minutes (if loaf browns too quickly, cover loosely with brown paper). Remove bread from oven and sprinkle with 3 tablespoons sugar. Cool on baking sheet 5 minutes, then transfer to rack and cool completely. *(Can be wrapped and stored at room temperature 2 days or frozen up to 1 month. Reheat thawed unwrapped loaf in 350°F oven 5 minutes.)*

Pulla (Finnish Cardamom Wreath)

Makes 2 wreaths

¼ cup warm water (105°F to 115°F)
1 envelope dry yeast
¾ cup sugar

1 13-ounce can (1⅔ cups) evaporated milk
3 eggs, room temperature
½ cup (1 stick) unsalted butter, room temperature
2 teaspoons salt
1 teaspoon crushed cardamom seeds

8 cups (about) all purpose flour
1 egg
2 tablespoons milk

¼ cup coarse crystal sugar (available at bakeries) and/or ¼ cup sliced almonds

Whipped Spiced Butter*

Combine water, yeast and 1 tablespoon sugar in large mixing bowl and stir until yeast is dissolved. Let stand until foamy and proofed, about 5 minutes.

Add remaining sugar, evaporated milk, 3 eggs, butter, salt and cardamom and mix well. Stir in 3 cups flour and beat until smooth. Gradually add remaining flour and mix until soft dough is formed. Cover and let stand at room temperature for 30 minutes.

Grease large bowl. Turn dough out onto lightly floured work surface and knead until smooth, satiny and small blisters appear, about 10 minutes. Place in greased bowl and turn to coat entire surface. Cover and let rise in warm area (85°F) until doubled in volume, about 1 hour.

Turn dough onto lightly *oiled* work surface. Divide in half, then divide each half into thirds. Shape each piece into long strand by rolling between palms of hands and oiled surface until 36 inches in length. Combine 3 strands and braid together; trim ends to make them even.

Place 8-inch cake pan in center of large baking sheet or 14-inch pizza pan. Grease outside edges of cake pan. Wrap braid around pan to form wreath and pinch ends together to seal.

Roll dough trimmings to make strand about 12 inches long. Shape into bow and place over sealed part of wreath. Repeat to make second wreath.

Combine egg and milk and brush over dough. Let rise in warm area until doubled, about 45 minutes.

Preheat oven to 375°F. Brush dough again with egg wash and sprinkle with sugar and/or almonds. Bake until loaves are golden, about 30 to 35 minutes. (If dough goes over edge of pan during baking, place piece of foil beneath.) Cool slightly on racks.

Set warm wreath on serving board and place spiced butter in center.

*Whipped Spiced Butter

1 pound unsalted butter, room temperature
½ cup whipping cream

3 tablespoons powdered sugar
½ teaspoon freshly grated nutmeg
½ teaspoon ground cardamom

Using electric mixer, whip butter until fluffy, adding cream gradually. Whip in sugar, nutmeg and cardamom.

Spoon into large pastry bag fitted with rosette tip. Press onto 7- or 8-inch plate (or dish that fits in center of bread wreath) to form domed spiral shape; finish with fancy design to decorate top.

Whipped spiced butter is also good on waffles, toast or nut breads.

Special Easter Bread

Enhanced with glacéed fruit and citrus peel, the dough for this bread is often shaped into a pair of doves in honor of the holiday.

Makes 2 loaves

¼ cup warm water (105°F to 115°F)
1 envelope dry yeast

½ cup milk
¾ cup sugar
½ cup (1 stick) unsalted butter, cut into 8 pieces

4 medium eggs, room temperature
1 teaspoon vanilla

1 teaspoon grated lemon peel
1 teaspoon grated orange peel
3½ to 4 cups all purpose flour

½ cup chopped glacéed fruit
½ cup raisins

1 egg yolk beaten with 2 tablespoons milk (glaze)
Sugar

Stir warm water and yeast in small bowl until yeast dissolves.

Heat milk in heavy medium saucepan. Add sugar and butter and stir until butter melts. Cool completely.

Beat eggs in large bowl until light in color. Blend in vanilla, lemon and orange peel. Stir in yeast mixture, cooled milk and 1½ cups flour using wooden spoon. Mix in enough of remaining flour to make soft dough. Turn dough out onto lightly floured surface. Knead in remaining flour a little at a time, then continue kneading until dough is smooth, about 10 minutes.

Grease large bowl. Combine glacéed fruit and raisins in small bowl (if shaping dough into doves, reserve 2 raisins for "eyes"). Sprinkle mixture with small amount of flour or sugar. Knead fruit into dough. Form into ball. Transfer to greased bowl, turning to coat entire surface. Cover with dry cloth. Let rise in warm draft-free area until doubled, 1½ to 2 hours.

Lightly butter and flour baking sheet. Punch dough down and divide in half. Shape each into oval for free-form loaves. Place on baking sheet. Or, form into doves: Set 1 half aside. Divide remaining half into 2 pieces. Form 1 piece into body of dove with pointed head, rounded body and slightly fanned-out tail. Set on baking sheet. Divide remaining piece in half. Shape into wings. Attach to sides of body. Repeat with remaining dough.

Cover dough with dry cloth. Let rise in warm draft-free area until doubled in volume, about 1 hour.

Preheat oven to 350°F. Brush dough with glaze. Sprinkle with sugar (if preparing doves, sprinkle sugar over body only; insert raisin in each for eye). Bake loaves 10 minutes. Cover loosely with foil and continue baking until toothpick inserted in center comes out clean, about 15 minutes. Cool completely. Break into wedges to serve. (*Breads can be prepared 2 days ahead. Store airtight.*)

Bran Molasses Sunflower Bread

Counterclockwise from top left: Ashton Idaho Rye; Peanut Butter Rye; Craggy Dark Bread; Parmesan Onion Rye; Feather Rye Rolls

Top and lower left:
A Sheaf of Wheaten Breadsticks
Bottom: Malted Crackers

Croissants

Irwin Horowitz

*American Chocolate
Bread: filling,
sealing and
dusting with sugar*

Christopsomo

This fragrant round loaf from Greece is studded with figs, walnuts and raisins and glazed with an orange syrup before baking. A decorative Greek cross adorns the top. Serve with butter, preserves and Greek-style coffee.

Makes 1 large round loaf

¾ cup (1½ sticks) unsalted butter
⅔ cup milk
½ cup orange or other fragrant honey
1½ teaspoons crushed mahlepi (mahleb)* *or* 1 teaspoon crushed aniseed and ½ teaspoon cinnamon
1 teaspoon salt
2 envelopes dry yeast
1 teaspoon honey
⅓ cup warm water (105°F to 115°F)
⅔ cup chopped dried figs
½ cup chopped walnuts
⅓ cup golden raisins
2 tablespoons all purpose flour

5 to 6 cups all purpose flour
2 teaspoons grated orange peel
3 eggs, room temperature

Orange Glaze
½ cup light corn syrup
¼ cup honey
¼ cup fresh orange juice
⅛ teaspoon crushed mahlepi (mahleb) *or* pinch of crushed aniseed and pinch of cinnamon

Milk
9 walnut halves

Heat butter with ⅔ cup milk and ½ cup honey in heavy small saucepan over low heat until butter melts, stirring to dissolve honey. Mix in mahlepi and salt. Cool to lukewarm. Meanwhile, stir yeast and 1 teaspoon honey into ⅓ cup warm water in large bowl. Cover with towel and let stand until foamy, about 5 minutes. Toss figs, walnuts and raisins with 2 tablespoons flour in separate bowl to coat.

Stir milk mixture, 2 cups flour and orange peel into yeast until smooth. Mix in eggs one at a time. Blend in remaining flour 1 cup at a time until soft, slightly sticky dough forms. Turn dough out onto lightly floured surface and knead in fruit mixture. Continue kneading until smooth and elastic, about 5 minutes. Butter large bowl. Add dough, turning to coat entire surface. Cover with plastic wrap and towel. Let rise in warm draft-free area until doubled, about 1¼ hours.

For glaze: Simmer corn syrup, honey, orange juice and mahlepi in heavy small saucepan over low heat 15 minutes. Cool to lukewarm.

Line baking sheet with parchment paper. Punch dough down. Turn out onto lightly floured surface and knead until smooth, 2 to 3 minutes. Let rest 10 minutes. Pinch off two 3-inch balls of dough and reserve. Knead remaining dough into smooth ball. Place in center of prepared baking sheet and flatten into 9-inch round. Roll each reserved dough piece into 14-inch rope. Cut 5-inch slit lengthwise in end of each rope, forming "Y." Brush milk across dough round in cross design. Place dough ropes on moistened marks. Curl cut ends outward, forming loops, to make Greek cross. Press walnut half in center of each loop, and one in center of crossed strips. Brush loaf with glaze (do not allow any glaze to drip underneath). Let rise in warm draft-free area until almost doubled in volume, about 30 minutes.

Position rack in lower third of oven and preheat to 350°F. Bake until loaf sounds hollow when tapped on bottom, about 45 minutes (if loaf browns too quickly, drape loosely with brown paper). Transfer to rack. Immediately brush with orange glaze. Cool 25 minutes; brush with glaze again. Cool completely. (*Can be wrapped tightly and stored at room temperature 3 days or frozen up to 1 month. Reheat thawed unwrapped loaf in 350°F oven 5 minutes.*)

*Ground seed of a wild, cherry-type fruit that originated in Persia. Available in Greek or Middle Eastern markets.

Grittibanz

These Swiss bread figures are decorated with everything from raisins, currants, almonds and walnuts to juniper berries and candied citron strips. More elaborate versions include vests, aprons and hats fashioned from the dough. Utterly charming and fun for the whole family to bake.

Makes 1 large figure

1¼ cups milk
½ cup (1 stick) unsalted butter
½ cup sugar
1 teaspoon vanilla
1 teaspoon salt
1 teaspoon grated orange peel
1 envelope dry yeast
½ teaspoon sugar
¼ cup warm water (105°F to 115°F)

2 eggs, room temperature, beaten to blend

½ teaspoon ground cardamom
5½ to 7 cups all purpose flour

Milk
Whole almonds

Raisins, hazelnuts, glacéed cherries (decoration)
1 egg beaten with 1 tablespoon milk and pinch of salt (glaze)

Heat 1¼ cups milk with butter in heavy saucepan over low heat until butter melts. Stir in ½ cup sugar, vanilla, salt and orange peel. Cool to lukewarm. Stir yeast and ½ teaspoon sugar into ¼ cup warm water in large bowl. Cover with towel and let stand until foamy, about 5 minutes.

Add milk mixture, eggs and cardamom to yeast. Blend in flour 1 cup at a time until soft, slightly sticky dough forms. Turn dough out onto lightly floured surface and knead until smooth and elastic, about 6 minutes, kneading in additional flour as necessary. Butter large bowl. Add dough, turning to coat entire surface. Cover bowl with plastic wrap and towel. Let dough rise in warm draft-free area until doubled in volume, about 1½ hours. (*Dough can also rise in refrigerator overnight. Punch down after 6 hours.*)

Punch dough down. Turn out onto lightly floured surface and knead until smooth, 2 to 3 minutes. Cover dough and let rest for 10 minutes.

To assemble, line large baking sheet with parchment paper. Form ⅔ of dough into 6 × 18-inch oval (for body of figure) and place on prepared sheet. Pull 1 end of oval to form neck. Roll ⅓ of remaining dough into ball and flatten to form head. Moisten 1 end with milk and attach to neck. Roll half of remaining dough into 14-inch-long rope for arms. Place under body near neck, moistening portion under body with milk. Arrange arms 3 inches from body at ends to allow for rising. Divide remaining dough in half and roll into two 12-inch-long ropes. Tie one loosely around neck as scarf and second around waist as belt. For boy figure, cut bottom of body ⅓ up and shape legs.* Arrange legs 5 inches apart at ends. Make indentations with blunt end of knife for cuffs on legs and arms. Using scissors dipped in flour, make ½-inch-deep snips to create hair. Decorate hems, cuffs, sleeve borders and hair with almonds, brushing with milk before attaching. Cover loosely with towel; let rise 15 minutes.

Meanwhile, preheat oven to 350°F. Just before baking, decorate face with raisin eyes, hazelnut nose and cherry mouth, brushing with milk to secure. Place raisin buttons down front of figure. Brush entire figure and decorations with egg glaze. Bake until figure is golden brown and sounds hollow when tapped on bottom, about 40 minutes. Cool 5 minutes on baking sheet. Transfer to rack and cool. Tie satin ribbon around neck before serving. (*Can be wrapped and stored at room temperature 3 days or frozen up to 1 month. Reheat thawed unwrapped bread in 350°F oven for 5 minutes.*)

*For girl, do not cut dough to shape legs. Uncut dough will bake to resemble skirt.

Pangiallo

Its name means "yellow bread," after its colorful components: candied citron, pine nuts and citrus peel. Accompany with tea or espresso.

Makes 1 round loaf

Bread Dough
1/3 cup golden raisins
1/4 cup dark raisins
3 tablespoons Marsala

1/2 cup milk
1/4 cup (1/2 stick) unsalted butter
1/4 cup sugar
1/2 teaspoon salt
1 envelope dry yeast
1/2 teaspoon sugar
1/4 cup warm water (105°F to 115°F)

1 egg
1 egg yolk
3 to 4 cups all purpose flour
1/2 teaspoon cinnamon
1/2 teaspoon freshly grated nutmeg

1/4 teaspoon ground cloves
1/4 teaspoon ground allspice
1/4 teaspoon ground aniseed
1/3 cup diced candied citron
1/3 cup chopped almonds, lightly toasted
1/3 cup pine nuts
2 teaspoons grated lemon peel
1 1/2 teaspoons grated orange peel

Spiced Syrup
1/4 cup light corn syrup
3 tablespoons water
2 tablespoons fresh orange juice
1/8 teaspoon cinnamon
1 tablespoon unsalted butter

Powdered sugar (optional)

For bread dough: Soak raisins in Marsala 20 minutes, stirring occasionally.

Heat milk with butter in heavy small saucepan over low heat until butter melts. Stir in 1/4 cup sugar and salt until dissolved. Cool to lukewarm. Meanwhile, stir yeast and 1/2 teaspoon sugar into 1/4 cup water in large bowl. Cover with towel and let stand until foamy, about 5 minutes.

Add lukewarm milk mixture to yeast. Beat in egg and yolk. Sift together 3 cups flour, cinnamon, nutmeg, cloves, allspice and aniseed. Mix several teaspoons of dry ingredients with candied citron, almonds and pine nuts in another bowl. Stir 2 cups dry ingredients into yeast mixture until smooth. Add raisin mixture and lemon and orange peels. Blend in remaining dry ingredients 1/2 cup at a time until soft, slightly sticky dough forms, adding more flour if necessary. Blend in nut mixture.

Turn dough out onto lightly floured surface and knead until smooth and elastic, about 5 minutes, kneading in additional flour as necessary. Butter large bowl. Add dough, turning to coat entire surface. Cover bowl with plastic wrap and towel. Let dough rise in warm draft-free area until doubled, about 2 hours.

For syrup: Simmer corn syrup, water, orange juice and cinnamon in heavy small saucepan over medium heat 5 minutes. Stir in butter. Cool.

Punch dough down. Turn out onto lightly floured surface and knead 4 minutes. Cover; let rest 10 minutes.

Line baking sheet with parchment paper. Shape dough into smooth, 2-inch-thick round. Transfer to prepared baking sheet. Brush top of loaf with spiced syrup, being careful not to let any drip under bread. Let rise until almost doubled in volume, about 45 minutes.

Preheat oven to 350°F. Brush top of loaf with syrup. Bake until loaf is golden brown and sounds hollow when tapped on bottom, about 40 minutes. Cool on rack 10 minutes. Brush bread with remaining syrup. Cool completely. Sift powdered sugar over loaf before serving, if desired. (*Can be wrapped and stored at room temperature 3 days or frozen 1 month.*)

Panpepato

*An orange-scented choco-
late icing crowns the top
of this loaf, but a simple
sprinkling of unsweetened
cocoa powder is an alter-
native finishing touch. For
best flavor, age the loaf
several days before serving.
Hard cheese, red wine, espresso or caffelatte are all
superb accompaniments.*

Makes 1 large round loaf

½ cup currants
½ cup golden raisins

1 envelope dry yeast
½ teaspoon sugar
¼ cup warm water (105°F to 115°F)

4 to 4½ cups all purpose flour
6 tablespoons (¾ stick) unsalted butter, chopped, room temperature
2 tablespoons grated orange peel
2 teaspoons freshly cracked pepper
1 teaspoon salt
1 teaspoon freshly grated nutmeg
¼ teaspoon ground cloves
1 cup warm water (105°F to 115°F)
½ cup honey
¼ cup olive oil
1 egg, beaten to blend

⅔ cup pitted dates, snipped into quarters

½ cup coarsely chopped almonds, lightly toasted
½ cup pine nuts
½ cup coarsely chopped walnuts
½ cup coarsely chopped semisweet chocolate
⅓ cup coarsely chopped glacéed orange peel
2 tablespoons all purpose flour
Olive oil

Bitter Chocolate Icing*

Cover currants and golden raisins with warm water and soak 20 minutes.

Stir yeast and ½ teaspoon sugar into ¼ cup warm water in small bowl. Cover with towel and let stand until foamy, about 45 minutes.

Place 4 cups flour in large bowl. Cut in butter until mixture resembles coarse meal. Mix in grated orange peel, pepper, salt, nutmeg and cloves. Make well in center of dry ingredients. Add 1 cup warm water, honey, olive oil and egg to yeast mixture and pour into well. Slowly stir liquid into flour, drawing flour from inner edge of well into center until all flour is incorporated and mixture forms smooth, slightly sticky dough. Turn dough out onto lightly floured surface and knead until smooth and elastic, about 10 minutes, kneading in additional flour as necessary if dough is sticky.

Drain currants and raisins. Combine in large bowl with dates, almonds, pine nuts, walnuts, chocolate and glacéed orange peel. Toss with 2 tablespoons flour. Knead fruit mixture evenly into dough. Brush large bowl with olive oil. Add dough, turning to coat entire surface. Cover bowl with plastic wrap and towel. Let dough rise in warm draft-free area until doubled in volume, about 1¼ hours.

Punch dough down. Turn out onto lightly floured surface and knead until smooth, 3 to 4 minutes. Cover dough and let rest for 10 minutes.

Brush 9-inch springform pan with olive oil. Line with parchment paper; brush paper with oil. Knead dough into smooth round. Set in prepared pan, flattening until dough touches sides. Cover loaf with kitchen towel. Let rise at room temperature until almost doubled, about 1 hour.

Position rack in center of oven and preheat to 350°F. Bake until bread is golden brown and sounds hollow when tapped on bottom, about 65 minutes. Cool 5 minutes in pan. Remove bread from pan and peel off parchment. Let loaf cool completely on rack. Spread warm bitter chocolate icing over top, allowing some to drizzle down sides. Let icing cool until set. Wrap bread with plastic or foil. Let stand 24 hours before using. (*Can be stored at room temperature up to 5 days.*) Slice into thin wedges to serve.

*Bitter Chocolate Icing

Makes about ½ cup

1 ounce unsweetened chocolate
2 tablespoons (¼ stick) unsalted butter

1 cup powdered sugar, sifted
1½ tablespoons hot water
1½ tablespoons orange liqueur

Melt chocolate and butter in top of double boiler set over hot water. Stir in sugar, hot water and liqueur until smooth. Use immediately.

Julekage (Norwegian Christmas Bread)

This bread traditionally is served with very thin shavings of gjetost (sweet caramel-colored goat cheese).

Makes three 8- or 9-inch round loaves

¼ cup warm water (105°F to 115°F)
2 envelopes dry yeast
½ cup sugar

2 cups warm milk (105°F to 115°F)
2 eggs, room temperature, beaten to blend
½ cup (1 stick) unsalted butter, melted
2 teaspoons salt
1 teaspoon crushed cardamom seeds (optional)
7 to 8 cups all purpose flour

1 cup diced mixed glacéed fruit
1 cup golden raisins

1 egg
¼ cup milk

¼ cup coarse crystal sugar (available at bakeries)
Almond Icing Glaze*
Additional glacéed fruits (optional decoration)

Combine water, yeast and 1 tablespoon sugar in large mixing bowl and stir until yeast is dissolved. Let stand until foamy and proofed, about 5 minutes.

Add remaining sugar, milk, 2 eggs, butter, salt and cardamom and mix well. Stir in 2 to 3 cups flour and beat until smooth. Gradually add remaining flour and mix until soft dough is formed. Cover and let rest 30 minutes.

Stir in glacéed fruit and raisins. Turn dough out onto lightly floured work surface and knead until smooth, springy and small blisters appear, about 10 minutes. Place in greased bowl and turn to coat entire surface. Cover and let rise in warm area (85°F) until doubled, about 1 hour.

Grease three 8- or 9-inch round pans. Turn dough out onto lightly *oiled* surface and divide into 3 parts. Shape each part into round loaf and place in prepared pans.

Combine egg and milk and brush some of mixture over top of loaves; reserve remainder. Let rise until almost doubled, about 45 minutes.

Preheat oven to 375°F. Brush loaves again with egg wash and sprinkle with coarse sugar. Bake until loaves are golden and sound hollow when tapped on bottom, about 25 to 30 minutes. If serving immediately, glaze and decorate with glacéed fruit. If preparing loaves ahead, glaze and decorate after reheating.

*Almond Icing Glaze

1½ cups powdered sugar, sifted
2 to 3 tablespoons whipping cream or half and half
½ teaspoon almond extract

Pinch of salt

Mix sugar with enough cream to make smooth icing. Add extract and salt.

St. Lucia Candle Crown and Lucia Buns

A beloved tradition in Sweden, these saffron-flavored breads are served on December 13, St. Lucia's Day, which begins the Christmas season.

Makes 1 wreath and 36 buns

¼ cup warm water (105°F to 115°F)
2 envelopes dry yeast
¾ cup sugar

1 13-ounce can (1⅔ cups) evaporated milk
3 eggs, room temperature, beaten to blend
2 teaspoons salt
¼ teaspoon powdered saffron *or* 1 teaspoon ground cardamom, ½ teaspoon freshly grated nutmeg and ¼ teaspoon turmeric

¾ cup (1½ sticks) unsalted butter, room temperature
7 to 7½ cups bread flour

½ cup golden raisins

1 egg
¼ cup milk

Additional raisins (decoration)

Combine water, yeast and 1 tablespoon sugar in large mixing bowl and stir until yeast is dissolved. Let stand until foamy and proofed, about 5 minutes.

Add remaining sugar, evaporated milk, 3 eggs, salt and saffron or mixed spices and blend well. Stir in butter and 3 cups flour and beat until smooth. Gradually add remaining flour and mix until soft dough is formed. Cover and let stand at room temperature for 30 minutes.

Grease large bowl. Turn dough out onto lightly floured work surface and knead until smooth, about 10 minutes. Knead in raisins. Place in greased bowl and turn to coat entire surface. Cover and let rise in warm area (85°F) until doubled, about 1 hour.

Dough will be easier to shape if it is now chilled 45 minutes or overnight.

Turn dough out onto lightly *oiled* work surface and divide into 3 parts.

For candle crown: Divide 1 part of dough into thirds. Shape each piece of dough into long strand by rolling between palms and oiled surface until 36 inches long. Combine strands and braid together; trim ends to make them even. Place braid on lightly greased baking sheet and shape into wreath about 7 inches in diameter. Pinch ends to seal. Roll dough trimmings to make strand about 12 inches long. Shape into bow and place over sealed part of wreath.

Combine egg and milk and brush over dough. Cover and let rise in warm area until doubled, about 45 minutes.

Preheat oven to 375°F. Brush dough again with egg wash. Bake until wreath is golden, about 20 to 25 minutes. Transfer to rack and let cool completely.

Press 4 red candles into wreath, spacing evenly. Use as centerpiece.

To Shape Lucia Buns

For Lucia cats: Divide 1 part of dough in half, then divide one half into 12 pieces (reserve second half for golden oxen). Shape each piece into strand about 8 inches long. Curl into S-shape making tight coil on each end. Press raisin into each coil. Place on lightly greased baking sheet(s). Brush egg wash over each bun. Cover and let rise in warm area until doubled, about 45 minutes.

Preheat oven to 375°F. Bake until golden, about 15 minutes. Serve warm.

For golden oxen: Divide 1 part of dough in half (or use part of dough as described with Lucia cats), then divide 1 half into 12 pieces. Shape each piece into strand about 10 inches long. Form strand into V-shape, curling ends outward to resemble horns. Place on lightly greased baking sheet(s).

Brush egg wash over each bun. Cover and let rise in warm area until doubled in volume, about 45 minutes.

Preheat oven to 375°F. Bake until golden, about 15 minutes. Serve warm.

For golden chariots: Divide ⅓ of dough into 24 parts. Roll each into strand about 12 inches long. Cross 2 strands to make symmetrical (X) design. Curve ends of dough so strands go in same direction. Press raisin into each coil. Place on lightly greased baking sheet(s). Brush egg wash over each bun. Cover and let rise in warm area until doubled, about 45 minutes.

Preheat oven to 375°F. Brush egg wash over dough. Bake until buns are golden, about 15 minutes. Serve warm.

Spanish King's Bread

A traditional double-braided ring found throughout Spanish-speaking countries and exchanged on Twelfth Night. Studded with candied citron, nuts and raisins and scented with mace, lemon peel and saffron, the finished loaf is glazed and decorated, then tied with a beautiful ribbon. Hidden inside the ring is an almond or a shiny new foil-wrapped coin symbolizing good luck for the one who finds it.

Makes 1 large ring

⅓ cup milk
¼ cup (½ stick) unsalted butter
⅓ cup sugar
½ teaspoon salt
¼ teaspoon saffron threads, crushed
1 tablespoon dry yeast
½ teaspoon sugar
¼ cup warm water (105°F to 115°F)

2½ to 3½ cups all purpose flour
1 tablespoon grated lemon peel
¾ teaspoon mace
2 eggs, room temperature, beaten to blend
2 egg yolks, room temperature
½ cup coarsely chopped walnuts

⅓ cup golden raisins
⅓ cup coarsely chopped candied citron
2 tablespoons finely ground walnuts

Milk
1 whole almond or foil-wrapped coin (optional)

1 egg beaten with 1 tablespoon milk
Powdered Sugar Glaze*
Walnut halves and candied citron (decoration)

Heat ⅓ cup milk with butter in heavy small saucepan over low heat until butter melts. Remove from heat. Stir in ⅓ cup sugar, salt and saffron. Cool to lukewarm. Stir yeast and ½ teaspoon sugar into ¼ cup warm water in large bowl. Cover with towel and let stand until foamy, about 5 minutes.

Add milk mixture, 1¼ cups flour, lemon peel and mace to yeast. Mix in eggs, half at a time, then beat in yolks until smooth. Toss chopped walnuts, raisins and citron with finely ground walnuts to coat. Mix into batter. Blend in remaining flour ½ cup at a time until soft, slightly sticky dough forms. Turn dough out onto lightly floured surface and knead until smooth and elastic, about 5 minutes, kneading in additional flour as necessary. Butter large bowl. Add dough, turning to coat entire surface. Cover bowl with plastic wrap and towel. Let dough rise in warm draft-free area until doubled in volume, about 1½ hours.

Punch dough down. Turn out onto lightly floured surface. Divide dough in half. Knead each half until smooth. Cover and let rest 10 minutes.

Line baking sheet with parchment paper. Roll each piece of dough into 20-inch-long rope. Moisten 1 end of each rope with milk and pinch moistened ends together. Twist ropes together loosely. Place on prepared baking sheet. Brush ends with milk and join together in ring, pinching together to seal. Widen center space of ring by pulling gently. Press whole almond into dough from underside, hiding completely. Cover bread with towel. Let rise at room temperature until almost doubled, 35 to 40 minutes.

Preheat oven to 350°F. Brush egg mixture over entire loaf, being careful not to let any run underneath. Bake until loaf is golden brown and sounds hollow when tapped on bottom, about 30 minutes. Cool 5 minutes on baking sheet, then cool completely on rack. Spread with Powdered Sugar Glaze, allowing some to drizzle down sides.

Press nuts and candied citron into icing. (*Can be wrapped and stored at room temperature 2 days or frozen 1 month.*)

*Powdered Sugar Glaze

Makes about ⅓ cup

1 cup powdered sugar, sifted
1 tablespoon fresh lemon juice

½ to 1 tablespoon milk

Mix powdered sugar, lemon juice and enough milk to make smooth glaze.

Three Kings Bread

In Mexico children get presents on January 6, Three Kings Day, and this rich holiday bread is traditional fare. An unshelled almond, ring or coin is baked into the bread; whoever gets the prize is assured good luck in the coming year.

Makes 1 large ring

⅓ cup warm water (105°F to 115°F)
2 eggs, room temperature
2 tablespoons nonfat dry milk powder
1 envelope dry yeast

2½ cups all purpose flour
½ teaspoon salt
½ cup (1 stick) unsalted butter
⅓ cup sugar

1 cup chopped mixed glacéed fruit
1 "prize" (such as a coin wrapped in foil)
1 egg white
2 to 3 tablespoons sugar

Powdered Sugar Icing*
Additional glacéed fruit (decoration)

Combine water, eggs, dry milk and yeast and stir until well mixed. Let stand until bubbly, about 5 minutes.

Measure flour into large mixing bowl; stir in salt. Using pastry blender, fork or 2 knives, cut in butter until mixture resembles coarse crumbs. Add sugar and stir to mix well.

Add yeast mixture and fold together until ingredients are blended and look like pastry dough; *do not overmix.* Using hands, press dough to form ball. Cover and refrigerate from 8 to 24 hours.

Lightly flour work surface. Roll pastry to form rectangle about 8 inches wide and 24 inches long. Sprinkle with glacéed fruit and place prize on dough. Roll dough lengthwise jelly roll fashion. Place seam side down on lightly greased baking sheet and shape into ring; press ends together to seal. Brush top with unbeaten egg white and sprinkle with sugar. Cover and let rise in warm area (85°F) until puffy but not quite doubled, about 1 hour.

Preheat oven to 375°F. Bake ring until golden, about 25 to 30 minutes. Transfer to wire rack and let cool completely. Decorate with icing and sprinkle with additional glacéed fruit.

*Powdered Sugar Icing

1 cup powdered sugar
1 teaspoon unsalted butter, room temperature

½ teaspoon lemon extract
Pinch of salt
1½ tablespoons (about) milk

Blend sugar, butter, lemon, extract and salt with just enough milk to make smooth, spreadable icing.

Appenzeller Birnbrot

This filled bread is best aged for one week or longer, and it makes an ideal gift: Wrap each baked log in crisp clear cellophane "firecracker" fashion and tie the ends with red satin bows.

Makes 2 loaves

Filling

1¼ cups water
1 pound dried pears, coarsely chopped
8 ounces pitted prunes, coarsely snipped
⅔ cup dried figs, coarsely chopped
¾ cup dry red wine
⅔ cup sugar
⅓ cup golden raisins
⅓ cup dark raisins or currants
2 tablespoons fresh lemon juice
2 teaspoons grated lemon peel
⅓ cup kirsch or pear brandy
½ teaspoon cinnamon
½ teaspoon freshly grated nutmeg
½ teaspoon ground cardamom
¼ teaspoon mace
⅔ cup coarsely chopped walnuts

Bread Dough

¾ cup milk
6 tablespoons (¾ stick) unsalted butter
½ cup sugar
1 teaspoon salt
1 envelope dry yeast
¼ teaspoon sugar
¼ cup warm water (105°F to 115°F)

2 eggs, room temperature, beaten to blend
1½ teaspoons grated lemon peel
5 to 6 cups all purpose flour

Milk

1 egg beaten with 1 tablespoon milk (glaze)

For filling: Bring 1¼ cups water to simmer in heavy large nonaluminum saucepan. Add pears, prunes and figs. Simmer gently until fruit is soft enough to mash with fork and water is absorbed, stirring frequently, about 35 minutes. Mix in wine, sugar, raisins, lemon juice and peel. Cook until mixture thickens to jam consistency, about 10 minutes, stirring frequently. Add kirsch, cinnamon, nutmeg, cardamom and mace and stir until liquid is absorbed, about 5 minutes. Mix in walnuts; cool. Cover filling and let stand at room temperature overnight.

For dough: Heat milk with butter in heavy small saucepan over low heat until butter melts. Stir in ½ cup sugar and salt until dissolved. Cool to lukewarm. Meanwhile, stir yeast and ¼ teaspoon sugar into ¼ cup warm water in large bowl. Cover with towel and let stand until foamy, about 5 minutes.

Add lukewarm milk mixture to yeast. Stir in eggs one at a time, using wooden spoon. Add lemon peel. Blend in flour 1 cup at a time until soft, slightly sticky dough forms. Turn dough out onto lightly floured surface and knead until smooth and elastic, about 4 minutes, kneading in additional flour as necessary. Butter large bowl. Add dough, turning to coat entire surface. Cover with plastic wrap and towel. Let rise in warm draft-free area until doubled, about 1¼ hours.

Punch dough down. Turn out onto lightly floured surface and knead until smooth, 1 to 2 minutes. Divide dough in half. Cover and let rest 10 minutes.

To assemble, line 2 baking sheets with parchment paper. Roll 1 piece of dough into 12-inch square on lightly floured surface. Fold dough into quarters. Transfer to sheet of waxed paper; unfold dough. Spread half of filling evenly over dough to within 1 inch of edges. Fold in 2 opposite ends. Starting with unfolded side, roll dough up jelly roll fashion using waxed paper as aid. Brush seam with milk and pinch to seal. Transfer loaf to prepared baking sheet, seam side down. Repeat with remaining dough and filling. Prick loaves with fork in diagonal stripes, spacing 1 inch apart. Cover each loaf with kitchen towel. Let rise at room temperature until almost doubled in volume, about 20 minutes.

Position rack in lower third of oven and preheat to 350°F. Brush loaves with egg glaze. Bake until top and bottom are golden brown, about 35 minutes. Cool 10 minutes on baking sheets, then cool completely or racks. Wrap each loaf with plastic or foil. Let stand 24 hours before slicing. *(Can be stored at room temperature up to 10 days.)*

Danish Cinnamon Marzipan Kringle

If oven is smaller than standard size, divide dough into two parts. This will allow better air circulation and more even baking. Make square 12 inches and roll filled dough about 18 inches long. Baking time is the same.

Makes 1 large loaf or 2 smaller loaves

1 cup whipping cream, room temperature
½ cup warm milk (105°F to 115°F)
3 egg yolks, room temperature, beaten to blend
1 envelope dry yeast
1 tablespoon sugar

3½ cups all purpose flour
¼ cup sugar
1 teaspoon salt
½ cup (1 stick) chilled unsalted butter

Filling
1 cup almond paste
½ cup chopped almonds
½ cup sugar
1 egg white
1 teaspoon cinnamon
1 teaspoon almond extract

Topping
Sugar
1 egg white, beaten
¼ cup sliced almonds

Combine cream, milk, egg yolks, yeast and 1 tablespoon sugar in small bowl and mix well. Let stand until foamy and proofed, about 10 minutes. Blend flour, ¼ cup sugar and salt in large mixing bowl. Cut in butter until pieces are about the size of small beans. Fold in yeast mixture just until ingredients are moistened. Cover with plastic wrap and refrigerate 12 to 24 hours.

For filling: Combine all ingredients in bowl and blend thoroughly.

Remove dough from refrigerator. Dust with flour and knead lightly in bowl until dough is smooth. Place on chilled marble slab, lightly floured pastry cloth or board and flatten dough by rapping with rolling pin 5 or 6 times in each direction. Roll into 24-inch square.

Spread filling to within 1 inch of edges. Roll up dough as tightly as possible.

For topping: Sprinkle sugar on work surface. Using rocking motion, roll dough with palms to form cylinder between 36 and 38 inches long. Place on lightly greased baking sheet and form into large pretzel. Brush with egg white and sprinkle with additional sugar and almonds. Cover and let rise in warm area (85°F) for 45 minutes (dough will look puffy but will not double).

Preheat oven to 375°F. Bake until loaf is golden, about 25 to 30 minutes. Remove from baking sheet. Serve warm.

Potica (Slovenian Filled Christmas Bread)

Makes two 9 × 5-inch loaves

¼ cup warm water (105°F to 115°F)
1 tablespoon dry yeast
½ cup warm milk (105°F to 115°F)

½ cup (1 stick) unsalted butter, room temperature
⅓ cup sugar
2 eggs, room temperature
1 teaspoon salt
4 cups all purpose flour

Filling
12 ounces walnuts, ground (3 cups)
¾ cup evaporated milk
¾ cup sugar
⅓ cup honey
½ teaspoon vanilla

Combine water and yeast in large mixing bowl and stir until yeast is dissolved. Add milk and let stand until foamy and proofed, about 5 minutes.

Lightly grease large bowl. Add butter, sugar, eggs, salt and half the flour to yeast mixture and beat until smooth. Add remaining flour and mix until soft dough forms. Knead by hand for about 10 minutes or with dough hook for 5 minutes. Place in greased bowl and turn to coat entire surface. Cover and let rise in warm area (85°F) until doubled in volume, about 1 hour.

For filling: While dough rises, combine walnuts, evaporated milk and sugar in saucepan. Stir in honey. Bring to boil, stirring constantly, and let boil 1 minute. Remove from heat and add vanilla. Cover and let cool to about 100°F.

Prepare work surface by covering with flannel-lined plastic cloth.

Grease two 9 × 5-inch loaf pans. Do not punch dough down but turn out onto work surface. Stretch into rectangle about 20 × 70 inches. Trim to 18 × 68 inches. Spread filling over dough to within ½ inch of edges. Starting from narrow end, roll into compact loaf. Cut in half and place in prepared pans. Let rise in warm area until doubled.

Preheat oven to 350°F. Bake loaves until golden brown, about 45 minutes. Remove from pans and let cool on racks. Slice and serve warm.

Makos Patko (Hungarian Poppy Seed Bread)

Delicious at breakfast with a mug of hot chocolate spiced with cinnamon.

Makes 1 loaf

Filling

1 cup (about 5 ounces) poppy seeds
1 cup boiling water

½ cup (1 stick) unsalted butter, room temperature
½ cup honey
½ cup sugar
⅔ cup raisins or currants
½ cup finely chopped walnuts
⅓ cup apple butter
2 teaspoons grated lemon peel
2 teaspoons grated orange peel
½ teaspoon cinnamon

Bread Dough
½ cup (1 stick) unsalted butter

¼ cup milk
¼ cup honey
1 envelope dry yeast
1 teaspoon honey
¼ cup warm water (105°F to 115°F)

2 to 3 cups all purpose flour
1 teaspoon grated orange peel
½ teaspoon salt
2 egg yolks

Milk

1 egg beaten with 1 tablespoon water
Vanilla Sugar Glaze*
¼ cup coarsely chopped walnuts

For filling: Cover poppy seeds with 1 cup boiling water. Soak overnight.

Pour poppy seed mixture into small saucepan and simmer over low heat 10 minutes. Drain through very fine sieve or in strainer lined with coffee filter. Spread poppy seed out on paper towel and pat dry. Grind poppy seed in batches to paste using mortar and pestle. Cream butter, honey and sugar in bowl until creamy. Stir in poppy seed, raisins, walnuts, apple butter, grated peels and cinnamon.

For dough: Heat butter with ¼ cup milk and ¼ cup honey in heavy small saucepan over low heat until butter melts, stirring to dissolve honey. Cool to lukewarm. Meanwhile, stir yeast and 1 teaspoon honey into ¼ cup warm water in large bowl. Cover and let stand until foamy, about 5 minutes.

Stir milk mixture, 1½ cups flour, orange peel and salt into yeast using wooden spoon. Blend in yolks one at a time. Mix in remaining flour ½ cup at a time until soft, slightly sticky dough forms. Turn dough out onto lightly floured surface and knead until smooth and elastic, about 6 minutes, kneading in additional flour as necessary. Butter large bowl. Add dough, turning to coat entire surface. Cover bowl with plastic wrap and towel. Let dough rise in warm draft-free area until doubled, about 1½ hours.

Punch dough down. Turn out onto lightly floured surface and knead until smooth, 1 to 2 minutes. Cover dough and let rest for 10 minutes.

Line large baking sheet with parchment paper. Roll dough out into 12 × 16-inch rectangle. Roll up on rolling pin and unroll onto lightly floured kitchen towel. Gently spread poppy seed filling over dough, leaving 1-inch border. Fold shorter ends in over filling. Roll up tightly jelly roll fashion, starting with 1 long edge and using towel as aid. Brush seam with milk and pinch to seal. Place roll on prepared baking sheet, seam side down. Cover with kitchen towel. Let rise at room temperature until almost doubled in volume, about 30 minutes.

Preheat oven to 350°F. Brush roll with egg mixture. Bake until top and bottom are golden brown, about 45 minutes (if loaf browns too quickly, cover loosely with brown paper). Cool 15 minutes. Spread loaf with vanilla sugar glaze and sprinkle with chopped nuts. Cool completely on rack. *(Can be prepared ahead. Wrap tightly and store at room temperature 4 days or freeze up to 1 month.)*

*Vanilla Sugar Glaze

Makes about ¼ cup

½ cup powdered sugar, sifted
1 tablespoon cornstarch
2 teaspoons brandy

1 teaspoon vanilla
1 to 3 teaspoons hot water

Mix powdered sugar, cornstarch, brandy, vanilla and enough hot water to make smooth, spreadable glaze.

Russian Krendl

An oversized pretzel-shaped loaf enclosing a spiced fruit filling.

Makes 1 large loaf

Filling
2 tablespoons (¼ stick) unsalted butter
1 large Golden Delicious apple, peeled and thinly sliced
2 tablespoons sugar
¾ cup apple juice
⅔ cup dried apples, cut into ½-inch pieces
⅓ cup dried apricots, cut into thirds
⅓ cup pitted prunes, cut into quarters
¼ cup vodka

Bread Dough
½ cup half and half
¼ cup (½ stick) unsalted butter
3 tablespoons sugar

1½ teaspoons vanilla
½ teaspoon salt
1 envelope dry yeast
½ teaspoon sugar
¼ cup warm milk (105°F to 115°F)

2 egg yolks
3 to 3½ cups all purpose flour

1 tablespoon unsalted butter, room temperature
1½ tablespoons sugar mixed with ½ teaspoon cinnamon
Milk

Vanilla Icing*
⅓ cup sliced almonds, lightly toasted

For filling: Melt butter in heavy large skillet over medium heat. Stir in apple slices and sugar and sauté until apples are tender, about 8 minutes. Stir in apple juice, dried apples, apricots and prunes. Cover and simmer gently until fruit is very soft, about 35 minutes. Add vodka and stir over medium heat until liquid is absorbed and mixture has jamlike consistency, about 5 minutes. Cool to room temperature. *(Can be prepared 1 day ahead. Cover with plastic wrap and store at room temperature.)*

For dough: Heat half and half with ¼ cup butter in heavy small saucepan over low heat until butter melts. Stir in 3 tablespoons sugar, vanilla and salt. Cool to lukewarm. Meanwhile, stir yeast and ½ teaspoon sugar into warm milk in large bowl. Cover and let stand until foamy, about 5 minutes.

Add half and half mixture to yeast. Stir in yolks. Mix in flour 1 cup at a time until soft, slightly sticky dough forms. Turn dough out onto lightly floured surface and knead until smooth and elastic, about 8 minutes, kneading in additional flour as necessary. Butter large bowl. Add dough, turning to coat entire surface. Cover with plastic wrap and towel. Let dough rise in warm draft-free area until doubled in volume, about 1¼ hours.

Punch dough down. Turn out onto lightly floured surface and knead until smooth, 3 to 4 minutes. Cover dough and let rest for 10 minutes.

To assemble, line baking sheet with parchment paper. Roll dough out on lightly floured surface into 10 × 32-inch rectangle. Roll dough up on rolling pin and unroll onto lightly floured towel. Spread 1 tablespoon butter over dough, leaving 1-inch border. Sprinkle cinnamon sugar over butter. Spread filling evenly over sugar. Roll dough up tightly jelly roll fashion, starting with 1 long side and using towel as aid. Brush seam and ends with milk and pinch to seal. Transfer roll to prepared baking sheet seam side down. Shape into pretzel by crossing ends and tucking under center of roll. Widen openings in pretzel to 4-inch diameter by pulling dough gently. Pat dough to flatten slightly. Cover with towel. Let rise in warm draft-free area until almost doubled, about 35 minutes.

Preheat oven to 350°F. Bake bread until golden brown on top and bottom, about 45 minutes (if loaf browns too quickly, cover loosely with brown paper). Transfer Krendl to rack and cool to lukewarm. Glaze with vanilla icing, allowing some to drizzle down sides. Sprinkle with almonds. Cool. *(Can be wrapped and stored at room temperature 3 days or frozen up to 1 month.)*

*Vanilla Icing

Makes about ¼ cup	½ cup powdered sugar, sifted 1½ tablespoons milk	½ teaspoon vanilla

Mix all ingredients until smooth.

Tolly's Cinnamon Rolls

Makes about 16	¾ cup warm water (105°F to 115°F) 2 envelopes dry yeast 1⅔ cups warm milk (105°F to 115°F) ¼ cup solid vegetable shortening ¼ cup sugar 1 tablespoon salt 6½ to 7 cups sifted all purpose flour ¼ cup (½ stick) butter, room temperature ¾ cup firmly packed brown sugar	¾ cup chopped walnuts or pecans ⅓ cup raisins 1½ teaspoons cinnamon *Icing* 2 cups powdered sugar ¼ to ⅓ cup fresh orange juice ¼ cup (½ stick) butter, room temperature ½ teaspoon vanilla ½ teaspoon almond extract

Oil large bowl and set aside. Pour warm water into large mixing bowl. Sprinkle with yeast and stir to dissolve. Blend in milk, shortening, sugar and salt. Add 3 cups flour and beat until smooth. Add enough remaining flour to form workable dough. Turn dough out onto lightly floured surface and knead until smooth and elastic, about 5 minutes. Transfer dough to oiled bowl, turning to coat all surfaces. Cover with damp towel and let stand in warm draft-free area until doubled, about 1 hour.

Grease 2 large baking sheets. Punch dough down. Turn out onto lightly floured surface and roll out into 12 × 18-inch rectangle. Spread with butter. Sprinkle evenly with brown sugar, nuts, raisins and cinnamon. Starting from 1 long edge, roll dough up as for jelly roll. Cut into slices slightly over 1 inch thick. Arrange on prepared baking sheets, tucking ends of dough under. Let stand in warm draft-free area until doubled in volume, about 40 minutes.

Preheat oven to 350°F. Bake rolls until golden, about 25 to 30 minutes.

Meanwhile, prepare icing: Combine all ingredients in small bowl of electric mixer and beat at high speed until smooth, using only enough orange juice to form spreadable icing. Frost rolls while still hot. Serve warm or at room temperature.

Cinnamon Brioche

Makes 12

⅓ cup sugar
1 ounce fresh yeast
9 eggs, room temperature
2½ teaspoons salt
2⅔ cups all purpose flour
2⅔ cups unbleached all purpose flour
1½ cups (3 sticks) butter, room temperature

2 eggs, beaten to blend (glaze)
¾ cup sugar mixed with
 1½ tablespoons cinnamon
¾ cup coarsely ground walnuts

1 cup powdered sugar mixed with
 3 tablespoons milk

In large bowl of heavy-duty mixer fitted with dough hook, blend ⅓ cup sugar and yeast to paste. Add 9 eggs and salt and mix until just incorporated. Add flours all at once and mix until dough comes together. Add butter in walnut-size pieces and knead with mixer at medium speed until dough is smooth and elastic, about 15 minutes. (Dough can also be made by hand.)

Oil large bowl. Transfer dough to bowl, turning to coat entire surface. Dust top lightly with flour. Cover with plastic wrap. Let rise in warm draft-free area until doubled in volume, about 1 hour.

Punch dough down in bowl. Cover with plastic wrap and refrigerate overnight.

Shape dough into square. Roll out on lightly floured surface into 18 × 31-inch rectangle about ¼ inch thick. Brush lightly with some of glaze. Sprinkle with cinnamon sugar. Sprinkle walnuts over top. Starting from 1 short edge, roll dough up as for jelly roll. Brush seam with glaze to seal. Cut roll into twelve 1½-inch-thick slices. Arrange on baking sheets cut side down, spacing 2 inches apart. Let rise in warm draft-free area until puffed, about 1 hour.

Preheat oven to 425°F. Brush rolls with glaze. Bake until golden brown, about 15 minutes. Immediately brush with powdered sugar and milk mixture and serve.

Cinnamon Rolls

These light, crisp-crusted rolls are best served shortly after baking.

Makes 2 dozen

½ cup warm milk (105°F to 115°F)
2 envelopes dry yeast
1 tablespoon grated lemon peel
1 teaspoon vanilla
¼ cup (½ stick) butter, room temperature
¼ cup sugar
2 eggs
½ teaspoon salt
3 cups all purpose flour
½ cup raisins

¾ cup sugar
¾ teaspoon cinnamon
¼ cup corn oil

Oil large bowl and set aside. Pour milk into small bowl. Sprinkle yeast over top. Let stand until foamy, about 5 minutes. Stir in lemon peel and vanilla. Cream butter and ¼ cup sugar in large mixing bowl. Add eggs and salt and beat until fluffy. Blend in yeast mixture. Add flour and raisins and mix well. Turn dough out onto floured surface and knead until smooth and elastic, about 5 minutes. Transfer to prepared bowl, turning to coat all surfaces. Cover with plastic wrap or damp towel. Let dough stand in warm draft-free area until doubled in volume, about 1½ hours.

Grease 2 large baking sheets. Combine ¾ cup sugar with cinnamon in small bowl and blend well. Punch dough down and turn out onto work surface. Divide evenly into 24 pieces. Shape each into ball. Dip into corn oil, then roll in cinnamon sugar. Arrange on prepared baking sheets. Let stand in warm draft-free area until doubled in volume, about 1 hour.

Preheat oven to 375°F. Bake cinnamon rolls until golden, about 20 minutes. Serve warm.

The Dog Team Tavern's Sticky Buns

Located in Middlebury, Vermont, The Dog Team Tavern has been serving these buns for over 40 years.

Makes 30

2 medium potatoes, boiled in at least 3 cups water, drained (reserve cooking water), peeled and mashed (1 cup)
½ cup sugar
½ cup (1 stick) butter or margarine, room temperature
1½ teaspoons salt
2 eggs
1 envelope dry yeast
7 cups (about) all purpose flour

2 cups firmly packed brown sugar
6 tablespoons water
3 cups chopped walnuts

½ cup sugar
2 teaspoons cinnamon
4 tablespoons (½ stick) butter, melted

Oil very large bowl and set aside. Combine 1 cup hot mashed potato, ½ cup sugar, ½ cup butter and salt in another large bowl and mix well. Cool to luke-warm. Add 1½ cups lukewarm potato water, eggs and yeast and beat until thoroughly blended. Stir in enough flour to make stiff dough. Turn out onto lightly floured surface and knead until smooth and elastic, about 8 to 10 minutes. Transfer to oiled bowl, turning to coat all surfaces. Cover bowl with greased plastic wrap. Let stand in warm draft-free area until doubled in volume, about 1½ hours. Punch dough down. Cover with greased plastic wrap and refrigerate until thoroughly chilled. (Dough can be prepared several days ahead to this point and refrigerated.)

Generously butter three 8-inch round pans. Spread bottoms with brown sugar, dividing evenly. Add 2 generous tablespoons water to each pan. Sprinkle 1 cup chopped walnuts over bottom of each pan.

Combine ½ cup sugar with cinnamon in 1-cup measure and mix well. Punch dough down; divide in half. Roll each half out on lightly floured surface into 10 × 16-inch rectangle about ¼ inch thick. Brush each rectangle with 2 table-spoons melted butter. Sprinkle with cinnamon sugar, dividing evenly. Starting at short end, roll dough up as for jelly roll. Cut each roll into 15 slices. Arrange 10 slices in each prepared pan. Let stand in warm draft-free area until doubled in volume, about 25 to 30 minutes. (If dough has been refrigerated for a long period, this will take several hours.)

Preheat oven to 350°F. Bake buns until golden brown, about 30 to 35 minutes. Immediately invert onto serving platters. Serve warm or at room temperature.

Pumpkin Biscuits

Makes 40

½ cup warm water (105°F to 115°F)
1½ envelopes dry yeast
Pinch of sugar
6¾ cups all purpose flour
1 cup milk, scalded and cooled
1 cup canned pumpkin
1 cup firmly packed light brown sugar

½ cup (1 stick) butter, melted
2 teaspoons ground ginger
1 teaspoon salt
½ teaspoon freshly grated nutmeg
¼ teaspoon *each* ground cinnamon, allspice and cloves

Generously grease large mixing bowl. Lightly grease baking sheet.

Combine water, yeast and sugar in another large bowl and let stand until foamy and proofed, about 15 minutes. Stir in flour, cooled milk, pumpkin, brown sugar, butter, ginger, salt and spices. Mix until soft dough forms. Transfer to floured work surface and knead until dough is smooth and elastic, about 10 minutes (or use dough hook of electric mixer and mix 8 to 10 minutes). Place dough in greased bowl, turning to coat entire surface. Cover and let rise in warm draft-free area until doubled, about 2½ hours.

Turn dough out onto floured work surface and roll to thickness of about 1 inch. Dip 2-inch biscuit cutter into flour and cut out biscuits. Arrange close together on prepared baking sheet. Cover and let rise until doubled in volume, about 45 to 60 minutes.

Preheat oven to 350°F. Bake until biscuits sound hollow when tapped on bottoms, about 25 minutes. Serve warm.

6 ❦ Savory Quick Breads, Muffins and Biscuits

Quick breads are a boon to busy cooks. Yeast loaves may be reserved for special occasions or leisurely weekends, but quick breads are exactly what their name indicates. Consider the Beer Bread on page 74: It contains four ingredients, takes five minutes to prepare and bakes while you put the rest of the meal together. Most other quick breads take just a bit longer, but 10- or 15-minute assembly is typical and baking time is usually less than an hour—for biscuits, far less.

And biscuits are the heart of this chapter. There are no less than 12 distinctive biscuit recipes, in addition to a couple of close relations— Cheese Scones (page 80) and an unusual Gruyère Shortbread (page 81). The variety is remarkable: You will find, for instance, oatmeal, rye, cheese, herb, sweet potato, and ham- or bacon-studded versions, to mention only some of the offerings. Then, too, there are savory muffins, garlic popovers, rustic soda breads . . . all prepared in minutes and meant to be enjoyed hot out of the oven.

Clancy's Irish Soda Bread

Makes 1 round loaf

1²/₃ cups milk, room temperature
1½ tablespoons fresh lemon juice
 ½ teaspoon baking soda
 3 cups all purpose flour
 2 tablespoons sugar
 1 tablespoons baking powder
 1 teaspoon salt
 1 cup dried currants
 1 teaspoon caraway seeds

¼ cup sugar
 1 teaspoon cinnamon
¼ cup (½ stick) butter, room
  temperature

Preheat oven to 350°F. Grease 9-inch pie pan. Combine milk and lemon juice in bowl. Let stand 5 minutes to sour. Stir in baking soda and let stand 2 minutes. Combine flour, 2 tablespoons sugar, baking powder and salt in large bowl. Stir in currants and caraway seed. Gradually add sour milk. Transfer dough to floured surface and knead until smooth, about 3 minutes.

  Form dough into ball and transfer to prepared pie pan, mounding to fit. Combine ¼ cup sugar and cinnamon in another small bowl. Sprinkle over top of dough. Bake until tester inserted in center comes out clean, about 45 minutes. Spread butter over top. Cool slightly. Serve warm.

Whole Wheat Soda Bread

Makes 1 round loaf

1 cup unbleached all purpose flour
2 tablespoons firmly packed brown
  sugar
1 teaspoon baking powder
1 teaspoon baking soda
½ teaspoon salt
2 tablespoons (¼ stick) butter, cut
  into pieces

2 cups whole wheat flour
¼ cup rolled oats
1½ cups buttermilk
  Melted butter

Preheat oven to 375°F. Grease baking sheet. Combine first 5 ingredients in large bowl. Cut in butter. Stir in whole wheat flour and oats. Make well in center, pour in buttermilk and stir until well moistened. Turn out onto floured board and knead *only* 1 minute. Shape into ball and place on baking sheet. Press into 6-inch circle and use sharp knife with floured blade to slash cross on top. Bake until loaf is nicely browned and sounds hollow when tapped, about 35 to 40 minutes. Transfer to rack and brush with butter. Serve warm.

Beer Bread

Makes one 9 × 5-inch loaf

3 cups self-rising flour
2 tablespoons sugar
1 12-ounce can beer, room
  temperature

7 tablespoons unsalted butter,
  melted

Preheat oven to 350°F. Combine flour and sugar in large bowl. Add beer and mix thoroughly. Pour into 9 × 5-inch loaf pan. Spoon 4 tablespoons melted butter evenly over top. Bake 20 minutes. Brush top with remaining butter. Continue baking until top is golden and tester inserted in center comes out clean, about 25 minutes. Serve warm.

❦ *Baking Soda and Baking Powder*

The most obvious advantage of these relatively modern leavening agents is that they work immediately. They demand speed; yeast requires patience. It is no surprise that the techniques for using them are very different.

Like yeast, baking soda and baking powder produce carbon dioxide. In contrast to the biological process of yeast, however, they depend on a chemical principle: carbon dioxide is produced when an acid and an alkali are combined with a liquid. They are used by being sifted with dry ingredients and added to liquids at the last minute before baking. The gases they produce expand in the heat of the oven, making breads and cakes rise.

Baking soda is an alkali. It is combined with acid liquids such as buttermilk or sour milk to effect the chemical process. These sour liquids—and strong flavors such as honey and spices—also balance its soapy taste.

Baking powder is a combination of alkali and acid. The alkali is baking soda. In single-acting baking powder the acid is cream of tartar. Double-acting baking powder, the type most frequently used today, replaces the cream of tartar with other acids. It is called double acting because it releases carbon dioxide at two points: when combined with liquid and in the presence of heat. When added it begins to work immediately and the batter should be put into the oven as soon as possible so that not too much gas escapes.

These leaveners should be stored in a dry place. Baking soda keeps almost indefinitely; baking powder begins to lose its potency once it is opened, so replace it every six months.

Dill-Beer Bread

Makes one 8 × 4-inch loaf

Glaze
- 1 egg
- ½ teaspoon salt

Bread
- 3 cups unbleached all purpose flour
- 3 tablespoons firmly packed light brown sugar
- 1 tablespoon plus 1 teaspoon baking powder
- 2 teaspoons dried dillweed
- 1½ teaspoons salt
- ½ teaspoon baking soda
- 1 12-ounce can beer, room temperature

Position rack in lower third of oven and preheat to 350°F. Generously grease 8 × 4 × 3-inch loaf pan and set aside.

For glaze: Insert steel knife into processor and mix egg with salt 4 seconds. Remove and set aside. Do not clean work bowl.

For bread: Combine flour, brown sugar, baking powder, dillweed, salt and baking soda in work bowl and mix 2 seconds. Add half of beer and blend using 4 on/off turns. Add remaining beer and mix using on/off turns just until batter is blended; *do not overmix.*

Transfer to prepared pan and brush top lightly with glaze. Bake until loaf is golden brown, about 45 minutes. Remove from pan and let cool on rack 10 minutes. Serve warm.

❦

Basil-Onion Bread

Makes one 12-inch loaf

1 large Spanish onion (12 ounces), quartered
½ cup plus 2 tablespoons vegetable oil

2 cups unbleached all purpose flour
1 tablespoon baking powder
1½ teaspoons salt
1 teaspoon baking soda

2 large green onions, including green tops, cut into 1-inch pieces
1 tablespoon fresh basil leaves
3 eggs
¼ cup sugar
¼ cup buttermilk
2 tablespoons apple cider vinegar

Generously grease 12 × 4-inch bread pan (8 to 10 cups). Sprinkle with flour, shaking off excess. Position rack in center of oven and preheat to 325°F.

Using food processor fitted with steel knife, mince onion in 2 batches using on/off turns. Wipe out work bowl. Heat oil in 1-quart saucepan over low heat. Add onion and cook 20 minutes, stirring occasionally; *do not brown.*

Combine flour, baking powder, salt and baking soda in work bowl and mix 3 seconds. Remove and set aside. Combine cooked onion, green onion and basil in work bowl and blend 3 seconds. Add eggs and sugar and mix 1 minute. Add buttermilk and vinegar and process 20 seconds. Add dry ingredients and blend using on/off turns just until flour is incorporated, stopping once to scrape down sides of bowl.

Spoon batter into prepared pan, spreading evenly. Bake until loaf is browned, about 40 to 45 minutes. Cool in pan 10 minutes. Turn out onto rack and let stand until completely cooled.

Date-Walnut Biscuit Bread with Caraway

This loaf is best served the day it is baked. The dough can also be made into individual biscuits.

Makes 1 round loaf

1 cup sifted unbleached all purpose flour
1 cup whole wheat flour
1½ teaspoons baking powder
½ teaspoon baking soda
½ teaspoon salt
2 tablespoons firmly packed dark brown sugar
½ teaspoon caraway seeds, lightly crushed

¼ cup (½ stick) unsalted butter, chopped, room temperature
½ cup coarsely chopped pitted dates
½ cup coarsely chopped walnuts
¾ cup buttermilk
1 egg

Position rack in center of oven and preheat to 375°F. Grease 9-inch cake pan. Sift flours, baking powder, baking soda and salt into medium bowl. Add any large pieces of wheat caught in sifter. Mix in sugar and caraway seeds. Cut in butter until mixture resembles coarse meal. Mix in dates and nuts. Make well in center. Blend buttermilk and egg. Add to well. Stir just until mixture is evenly moistened. Turn out onto well-floured surface and knead gently until smooth, about 20 times. Form dough into ball. Place in prepared pan; flatten to thickness of 1½ inches. Cut ⅓-inch-deep cross in top of dough. Bake until brown and firm to touch, 35 to 40 minutes. Cool slightly on rack. Serve warm.

Sour Cream Corn Muffins

You will find this recipe cooperative no matter what size muffin pans you have on hand.

Makes 24 mini, 12 regular or 6 extra-large muffins

1 cup yellow cornmeal
1 cup all purpose flour
¼ cup sugar
2 teaspoons baking powder
1½ teaspoons salt

½ teaspoon baking soda
1 cup sour cream
2 eggs
¼ cup (½ stick) butter, melted

Preheat oven to 425°F. Generously butter muffin cups. Mix cornmeal, flour, sugar, baking powder, salt and baking soda in medium bowl. Stir sour cream, eggs and melted butter in small bowl to blend. Add to dry ingredients and stir just until evenly moistened; do not overmix or muffins will be tough. Turn batter into prepared muffin cups, filling almost to top. Bake until muffins are light golden and tester inserted in centers comes out clean, about 10 to 15 minutes for mini, 15 to 20 minutes for regular and 25 to 30 minutes for extra-large muffins. Cool in pans 5 minutes before removing. Serve immediately.

Spiced Masa Corn Muffins

Makes 8

2 tablespoons fresh parsley leaves
1 cup unbleached all purpose flour
¾ cup plain yogurt
½ cup vegetable oil
7 tablespoons yellow instant masa mix or yellow cornmeal
2 eggs

¼ cup sugar
2 teaspoons baking powder
1 teaspoon dried red pepper flakes
½ teaspoon ground coriander
½ teaspoon baking soda
½ teaspoon salt
Butter

Position rack in center of oven and preheat to 375°F. Generously grease eight ½-cup muffin cups.

Using food processor fitted with steel knife, mince parsley. Add all remaining ingredients except butter and process 3 seconds, stopping once to scrape down sides of work bowl. Continue processing until just mixed, about 1 more second. Divide batter among prepared muffin cups. Bake until light brown, 20 to 25 minutes. Cool in pan 8 minutes. Serve corn muffins warm with butter.

Golden Garlic Clouds

Makes about 1 dozen popovers

5½ to 6 teaspoons solid vegetable shortening

1 cup all purpose flour
2 teaspoons bouquet garni seasoning, finely crushed
1 teaspoon salt

¼ teaspoon baking powder
4 eggs
1 cup milk
12 garlic cloves, crushed in garlic press

Position rack in lower half of oven and preheat to 450°F. Place ½ teaspoon shortening in each cup of cast iron popover pan or heavy muffin tin. Heat in oven until shortening is almost smoking, approximately 5 to 10 minutes.

Meanwhile, sift flour, seasoning, salt and baking powder in medium bowl. Beat eggs in large bowl of electric mixer until just foamy. Add milk and stir through. Add flour mixture to eggs and milk and mix until smooth. Stir in crushed garlic.

Fill popover cups about ⅔ full. Bake until popovers are puffed and tops are golden brown, about 20 to 25 minutes; do not open oven door for first 20 minutes. Serve popovers immediately.

Onion-Cheese Muffins

Makes 1 dozen

3½ cups all purpose flour
4 teaspoons baking powder
2 teaspoons salt
1 cup finely shredded cheddar cheese (3 ounces)
½ cup chopped green onion (4 medium)
2 tablespoons chopped fresh parsley

¾ to 1 teaspoon celery seeds
½ teaspoon Italian seasoning

1 cup plus 3 tablespoons milk
2 eggs
¼ cup vegetable oil
⅓ cup shredded cheddar cheese (1 ounce)

Preheat oven to 375°F. Generously grease muffin cups. Sift flour, baking powder and salt into large bowl. Add 1 cup cheese, green onion, parsley, celery seeds and Italian seasoning and toss to blend.

Beat milk, eggs and oil in small bowl to blend. Add to dry ingredients and stir only until flour mixture is evenly moistened (do not overmix or muffins will be tough). Spoon into prepared muffin cups, filling to top. Sprinkle with remaining ⅓ cup cheese. Bake until muffins are golden and tester inserted in centers comes out clean, about 30 minutes. Serve immediately.

Quick Processor Biscuits

Makes 1 dozen

2 cups all purpose flour
¼ cup (½ stick) butter, chilled and cut into thirds

2 teaspoons baking powder
¼ teaspoon salt
⅔ cup milk

Preheat oven to 450°F. Combine flour, butter, baking powder and salt in processor and blend using on/off turns until mixture resembles coarse meal, about 15 seconds. With machine running, add milk through feed tube and mix 7 seconds; *do not overmix.* Turn dough out onto lightly floured surface and knead gently 10 times. Roll dough to thickness of ½ inch. Cut into rounds using 2-inch floured biscuit or cookie cutter. Transfer rounds to baking sheet with sides almost touching. Bake until biscuits are golden, about 10 to 12 minutes. Serve hot.

Four ounces shredded cheddar or grated Parmesan cheese or ¼ cup finely diced crisply cooked bacon can be mixed with batter before milk is added.

Neighborhood Biscuits

Makes 1 dozen

Vegetable oil
2 cups self-rising flour
¼ cup dry buttermilk powder

¾ cup water
¼ cup vegetable oil

Preheat oven to 425°F. Pour oil into 9 × 13-inch baking dish to depth of about ⅛ inch. Combine flour and buttermilk powder in large bowl. Add water and ¼ cup oil and mix thoroughly. Turn dough out onto lightly floured surface and knead until smooth, about 30 seconds. Roll dough out to thickness of ½ inch. Dip 2½-inch cutter into flour, then cut out biscuits. Arrange close together in prepared dish, turning to coat with oil. Bake until golden, about 10 to 12 minutes. Serve biscuits hot.

Buttermilk Biscuits

These large, soft biscuits are a natural with butter and honey. Serve straight from the oven with fried chicken, barbecued ribs, or on their own.

Makes 6

2 cups sifted unbleached all purpose flour
2 teaspoons baking powder
¼ teaspoon baking soda

¼ teaspoon salt
6 tablespoons solid vegetable shortening, room temperature
1 cup buttermilk

Position rack in center of oven and preheat to 450°F. Sift flour, baking powder, baking soda and salt into medium bowl. Cut in shortening until mixture resembles coarse meal. Make well in center. Add buttermilk to well. Stir just until mixture is moistened.

Generously flour hands. Divide dough into 6 pieces. Lightly toss each piece back and forth between hands to form ball. Arrange on ungreased baking sheet. Flatten to 1-inch rounds; sides should touch. Bake until light brown, 18 to 20 minutes. Cool biscuits for 5 minutes on rack before serving.

Oatmeal Biscuits

A touch of coriander and orange peel makes all the difference in these classics. Serve hot with butter for breakfast, lunch or dinner.

Makes about 8

1½ cups sifted unbleached all purpose flour
2 tablespoons sugar
2½ teaspoons baking powder
½ teaspoon ground coriander
½ teaspoon salt
½ cup rolled oats
1 teaspoon grated orange peel

3 tablespoons unsalted butter, chopped, room temperature
3 tablespoons solid vegetable shortening, room temperature
¾ cup half and half
Additional half and half
Additional rolled oats

Position rack in center of oven and preheat to 450°F. Sift flour, sugar, baking powder, coriander and salt into medium bowl. Mix in ½ cup oats and orange peel. Cut in butter and shortening. Lightly rub mixture between fingertips until coarse meal forms. Make well in center. Add ¾ cup half and half to well. Stir just until mixture is evenly moistened. Turn out onto well-floured surface and knead gently just until dough holds together, about 12 times. Roll out gently to thickness of ¾ inch. Cut out rounds using 2½- to 3-inch floured cutter (push straight up and down; do not twist). Arrange on ungreased baking sheet, spacing ½ inch apart. Reroll scraps and cut out additonal rounds. Brush tops with half and half and sprinkle with oats. Bake until light brown, 10 to 12 minutes. Cool biscuits for 5 minutes on rack before serving.

Miniature Rye Biscuits

Serve these biscuits hot from the oven with plenty of butter. Their rustic character is ideal with hearty stews.

Makes 8

½ cup rye flour
½ cup all purpose flour
1 teaspoon unsweetened cocoa powder
1 teaspoon baking powder
¼ teaspoon baking soda
⅛ teaspoon salt
3 tablespoons chilled butter
⅓ cup buttermilk
2 teaspoons molasses
½ teaspoon aniseed

Preheat oven to 450°F. Sift dry ingredients into medium bowl. Cut in butter until mixture resembles coarse meal. Combine buttermilk and molasses in cup and blend well. Add to flour mixture with aniseed and stir until evenly moistened. Turn dough out onto lightly floured surface and knead lightly 10 to 15 times. Pat dough into ¾-inch-thick circle. Cut out biscuits using 1½-inch round cutter. Arrange on ungreased baking sheet. Bake until golden, 12 to 15 minutes. Serve biscuits warm.

Cheese Scones

An excellent accompaniment to chicken salad, fruit salad or smoked fish.

Makes 6

1¾ cups all purpose flour
2½ teaspoons baking powder
2 teaspoons sugar
½ teaspoon salt
½ cup grated cheddar cheese
¼ cup (½ stick) chilled unsalted butter
2 eggs, beaten to blend
⅓ cup whipping cream

Preheat oven to 450°F. Grease and flour baking sheet. Sift flour, baking powder, sugar and salt into large bowl. Cut in cheese and butter using pastry blender or 2 knives until mixture resembles coarse meal. Reserve 1 tablespoon beaten egg. Blend remaining egg with cream in small bowl. Mix into dry ingredients using fork. Turn dough out onto lightly floured surface and pat into 8-inch circle ¾ inch thick. Cut into 6 wedges. Arrange on prepared sheet. Brush tops with reserved egg. Bake until golden, about 15 minutes. Serve warm.

Elizabeth's Cheese Biscuits

These delicious biscuits are served hot with dinner at Elizabeth on 37th, a restaurant housed in a turn-of-the-century Savannah mansion.

Makes about 20

2 cups unbleached all purpose flour
⅓ cup nonfat dry milk powder
3 tablespoons grated white cheddar cheese (preferably raw milk)
2½ tablespoons wheat germ
2 tablespoons grated mozzarella cheese
2 tablespoons grated Emmenthal cheese
1 tablespoon baking powder
1 teaspoon salt
½ cup (1 stick) chilled butter, cut into 8 pieces
1 cup cold water

Preheat oven to 350°F. Lightly butter 2 baking sheets. Combine all ingredients except butter and water in large bowl of heavy-duty electric mixer. Using paddle attachment, cut in butter until mixture resembles coarse meal. Slowly pour in water, beating until dough just comes together. *(Dough can also be made by hand.)* Turn out onto lightly floured surface and pat to ¾-inch thickness. Cut into 2½-inch squares using floured knife. Arrange on prepared sheets, spacing 1 inch apart. Bake until light brown, about 15 minutes. Serve immediately.

❦

Gruyère Shortbread

2 servings

3 tablespoons butter, room
temperature
½ cup all purpose flour
¼ teaspoon salt

Pinch of ground red pepper
1 egg yolk
½ cup finely grated Gruyère cheese

Preheat oven to 350°F. Cream butter in medium bowl. Blend in flour, salt and red pepper. Add yolk and blend until dough forms ball. Mix in cheese.

Turn dough out onto baking sheet and form into 4-inch square ½ inch thick. Cut diagonally in both directions to form 4 triangles, separating triangles slightly with knife. Bake until golden, about 25 minutes. If dough spreads during baking, cut triangles apart with knife while hot. Cool on baking sheet 3 minutes, then transfer shortbread to rack. Serve warm.

Onion Rosemary Biscuits

Makes about 25

3 tablespoons bacon drippings
2 cups minced onion
1½ teaspoons dried rosemary,
crumbled
¾ teaspoon freshly ground pepper
¼ teaspoon salt

2¼ cups sifted unbleached all
purpose flour
1 tablespoon sugar

2½ teaspoons baking powder
½ teaspoon baking soda
½ teaspoon salt
5 tablespoons unsalted butter,
chopped, room temperature
5 tablespoons solid vegetable
shortening, room temperature
1 egg, beaten to blend
⅔ cup (about) buttermilk

Heat drippings in heavy large skillet over medium-low heat. Add onion, rosemary, pepper and ¼ teaspoon salt. Cook until onion is tender, stirring frequently, about 8 minutes. Cool.

Position rack in center of oven and preheat to 450°F. Sift flour, sugar, baking powder, baking soda and ½ teaspoon salt into medium bowl. Cut in butter and shortening until mixture resembles coarse meal. Make well in center. Place egg in measuring cup. Blend in enough buttermilk to measure ⅔ cup. Reserve ¼ cup onion mixture. Stir remainder into buttermilk. Add to well. Stir just until mixture is evenly moistened. Turn out onto well-floured surface and knead gently just until dough holds together, about 12 times. Roll out gently into rectangle ½ inch thick. Spread with reserved onion mixture. Cut into 1½ × 2½-inch rectangles, pushing straight down with floured sharp knife; do not use back-and-forth motion. Arrange on ungreased baking sheet, spacing ½ inch apart. Bake until golden brown, 12 to 14 minutes. Cool biscuits for 5 minutes on rack before serving.

Cream Biscuits

Fresh parsley accents these miniature savories from Seasons restaurant in The Bostonian hotel in Boston. A delightful accompaniment to seafood bisques and chowders.

Makes about 40

2²/₃ cups pastry flour
  1 tablespoon sugar
2½ teaspoons baking powder
  1 teaspoon salt

1½ cups whipping cream
  1 tablespoon melted butter
  1 tablespoon minced fresh parsley

Preheat oven to 375°F. Line baking sheets with parchment paper. Combine flour, sugar, baking powder and salt in large bowl. Add cream and mix with fork until soft dough forms. Divide dough in half. Roll or pat 1 portion out on lightly floured surface to thickness of ½ inch. Brush with melted butter. Sprinkle with parsley. Roll or pat remaining dough out to thickness of ½ inch. Set atop first half. Using 1-inch cutter or glass, cut into rounds. Arrange on prepared sheets. Bake until lightly colored, about 15 minutes. Serve immediately.

Herbed Baking Powder Biscuits

Makes about 20

Glaze
  1 egg
  ½ teaspoon salt

Biscuits
  ⅓ cup fresh parsley leaves
  2 large green onions, including green tops, cut into 1-inch pieces
  ⅛ teaspoon curry powder
  2 cups unbleached all purpose flour

6 tablespoons solid vegetable shortening or unsalted butter, chilled
  1 tablespoon baking powder
  2 teaspoons sugar
  1 teaspoon salt
  ⅔ cup milk
  2 teaspoons Dijon mustard

Position rack in center of oven and preheat to 450°F. Lightly grease baking sheet.

For glaze: Insert steel knife into processor and mix egg with salt until blended, about 4 seconds. Remove and set aside. Wipe out work bowl with paper towel.

For biscuits: Combine parsley, green onion and curry powder in work bowl and mince using 10 on/off turns. Add flour, shortening or butter, baking powder, sugar and salt and mix using on/off turns until shortening is size of small peas. Combine milk and mustard in small bowl. With machine running, pour mixture quickly into feed tube, stopping as soon as dough is mixed; *do not overmix.*

Turn dough out onto well-floured surface and roll out to thickness of ½ inch. Cut into rounds using 2-inch biscuit or cookie cutter. Transfer to baking sheet. (For soft-sided biscuits, rounds should be almost touching. For crustier biscuits, space 1 inch apart.) Brush glaze over tops. Bake until biscuits are golden, about 12 to 15 minutes. Serve warm.

Smoking Day Biscuits

Makes about 2 dozen

1 cup unbleached all purpose flour
1 cup cake flour (do not use self-rising)
4 teaspoons baking powder
½ teaspoon salt
¼ cup (½ stick) chilled unsalted butter, cut into 4 pieces

2 slices bacon, crisply cooked, drained and crumbled
2 small green onions, minced
⅔ to ¾ cup cold milk

Unsalted butter
Honey

Preheat oven to 425°F. Grease baking sheet and set aside. Combine flours, baking powder and salt in deep bowl and mix well. Cut in butter with pastry blender until mixture resembles coarse meal. Toss in bacon and green onion using fork. Add enough milk to make dough moist but not wet, tossing with fork until *just* blended; *do not overwork dough.*

Turn out onto floured board and *knead only once or twice.* Gently shape into rectangle ½ inch thick. Cut into squares and place ⅛ to ¼ inch apart on baking sheet. Bake until puffed and golden, 15 to 18 minutes. Serve immediately with unsalted butter and honey.

Ham Biscuits with Mustard Butter

Light biscuits flecked with bits of ham and parsley. Serve as an hors d'oeuvre or with breakfast or dinner.

Makes about 2 dozen

Mustard Butter
1 small garlic clove
½ cup (1 stick) unsalted butter, room temperature
1 tablespoon coarse-grained mustard
1½ teaspoons Dijon mustard
1 teaspoon fresh lemon juice

Biscuits
2 cups all purpose flour
1¾ teaspoons baking powder
½ teaspoon baking soda
½ teaspoon salt
⅓ cup solid vegetable shortening
¾ cup ¼-inch cooked ham cubes
2 tablespoons chopped fresh parsley
¾ cup buttermilk

Melted unsalted butter (about 1 tablespoon)

For butter: With machine running, drop garlic through feed tube of processor to mince. Add butter and mix using 3 to 4 on/off turns. Scrape bottom and sides of work bowl. Add mustards and lemon juice and mix well. Turn mustard butter into container with tight-fitting lid and refrigerate.

For biscuits: Preheat oven to 425°F. Lightly grease baking sheet. Mix flour, baking powder, soda and salt in processor. Add shortening and process using on/off turns until mixture resembles coarse meal. Turn into medium bowl. Mix in ham and parsley. Add buttermilk and stir with wooden spoon just until dough holds together; do not overmix.

Turn dough out onto lightly floured surface. Knead 3 to 4 times. Pat or lightly roll to ¾-inch thickness. Using 1½-inch cutter or standard biscuit cutter, press out biscuits. Gently reroll scraps. Transfer biscuits to prepared baking sheet, spacing evenly. Brush tops with melted butter. Bake until lightly browned, about 20 minutes.

Split each hot biscuit partially using fork. Insert piece of chilled mustard butter into each biscuit. Serve warm.

Sweet Potato Biscuits

Dense and fragrant biscuits that are perfect with turkey or ham.

Makes about 1 dozen

1 10- to 12-ounce sweet potato, baked, peeled and mashed

1½ cups sifted unbleached all purpose flour
2½ teaspoons baking powder
½ teaspoon cinnamon
½ teaspoon salt
¼ teaspoon allspice
¼ teaspoon freshly grated nutmeg
⅓ cup firmly packed dark brown sugar

½ teaspoon grated lemon peel
½ cup (1 stick) unsalted butter, chopped, room temperature
2 tablespoons whipping cream
1 egg blended with 1 tablespoon whipping cream (glaze)

Puree potato pulp in processor until smooth. Measure ¾ cup and set aside. Cool to room temperature.

Position rack in upper third of oven and preheat to 450°F. Sift flour, baking powder, cinnamon, salt, allspice and nutmeg into medium bowl. Mix in sugar and lemon peel. Cut in butter until mixture resembles coarse meal. Add ¾ cup sweet potato pulp and cream to well. Stir just until mixture is evenly moistened. Turn out onto lightly floured surface and knead gently just until dough holds together, about 12 times. Divide dough into 3 pieces. Gently pat each piece into ¾-inch-thick round. Cut into fourths, pushing straight down with floured knife; do not use back-and-forth motion. Arrange on ungreased baking sheet, spacing ½ inch apart. Brush tops with glaze. Bake until golden brown, about 12 minutes. Cool 5 minutes on rack before serving.

7 ❦ Sweet Quick Breads

So popular and numerous are sweet quick breads that they constitute the largest chapter of this book. While sweetened yeast breads are often Old World specialties, this section is where you will find such star-spangled American classics as Boston Brown Bread (page 86), date-nut loaves, and ever-popular banana, cranberry, pumpkin and zucchini breads. There is also a generous selection of fruit, nut and whole-grain muffins, as well as a sampling of sweetened biscuits and scones.

Many a home baker has built a reputation on these undemanding but thoroughly tempting quick breads. You, too, are assured of success if you follow one unbending rule: Do not overwork the batter. If they are to be tender and light rather than rubbery, quick breads must be mixed only enough to moisten the ingredients but not to develop the gluten in the flour. What could be simpler? These easy breads do not even allow you to linger over their preparation.

Remember this selection of recipes when you are planning breakfast or brunch, of course—but also any time you want to whip up a treat for the coffee or tea table, or for other informal entertaining. Keep in mind, too, that quick breads freeze perfectly, ready to be enlisted at the last minute as ideal gifts and greetings from your kitchen.

Boston Brown Bread

Makes 3 or 4 round loaves

2 cups graham flour
2 cups buttermilk
1 cup raisins
1/2 cup unbleached all purpose flour

1/2 cup molasses
2 teaspoons baking soda
1 teaspoon salt

Lightly grease three or four 1-pound cans (4 1/4 inches high). Combine all ingredients and mix well. Fill cans no more than 2/3 full. Let stand 30 minutes. Preheat oven to 350°F. Bake until tester inserted in center of loaves comes out clean, about 45 to 50 minutes. Let stand until cans are cool enough to handle. Remove bottom with can opener, run knife around inside and gently push out bread. Serve warm.

Bourbon Pecan Loaf

Makes one 8 1/2 × 4 1/2-inch loaf

2 cups all purpose flour
1 teaspoon baking powder
3/4 teaspoon baking soda
1/4 teaspoon salt
2 eggs
1/2 cup (1 stick) butter, room temperature

1/2 cup maple syrup
1/3 cup firmly packed dark brown sugar
1/2 cup buttermilk
1 cup chopped pecans
3 tablespoons bourbon

Preheat oven to 350°F. Generously grease 8 1/2 × 4 1/2-inch loaf pan. Line bottom and sides with waxed paper.

Sift flour, baking powder, baking soda, and salt into medium bowl and set aside. Combine eggs, butter, syrup and sugar in large bowl of electric mixer and beat at medium speed until light and fluffy. Reduce speed to low. Add flour mixture and buttermilk alternately to egg mixture, beating well after each addition. Stir in pecans and bourbon. Transfer batter to prepared pan, smoothing top. Bake until tester inserted in center comes out clean, about 65 minutes. Let cool in pan on rack 10 minutes. Remove loaf from pan and discard waxed paper. Let cool completely on rack before serving.

Welsh Tea Loaf

Makes two 9 × 5-inch loaves

2 3/4 cups water
1 15-ounce package raisins
4 teaspoons baking soda

1 1/2 cups (3 sticks) butter or margarine, room temperature
1 1/2 cups sugar

3 eggs
2 tablespoons molasses
1 tablespoon vanilla
1/8 teaspoon salt
4 cups all purpose flour

Preheat oven to 350°F. Grease two 9 × 5-inch loaf pans. Combine water and raisins in medium saucepan. Bring to boil over high heat. Reduce heat to low and simmer 2 minutes. Stir in baking soda. Let cool.

Meanwhile, cream butter with sugar in large bowl of electric mixer. Add eggs one at a time, beating well after each addition. Add molasses, vanilla and salt and continue beating until well blended, 2 to 3 minutes. Beat in flour. Add raisin mixture and beat on low speed until well blended, about 2 minutes. Spoon batter into prepared pans. Bake until tester inserted in centers comes out clean, 50 to 60 minutes. Cool in pans on rack. Serve at room temperature.

Bishop's Bread

Spread slices of this delicious bread with cream cheese or sweet butter, and serve with fresh fruit or chicken salad.

Makes one 9 × 5-inch loaf

2½ cups cake flour, sifted
½ cup sugar
4½ teaspoons baking powder
½ teaspoon salt
½ cup chopped walnuts
½ cup chopped dates

½ cup chopped candied orange peel
2 eggs
1 cup milk
¼ cup solid vegetable shortening
1 ounce unsweetened chocolate

Preheat oven to 350°F. Grease and flour 9 × 5-inch loaf pan. Combine cake flour, sugar, baking powder and salt in large bowl. Stir in walnuts, dates and orange peel. Beat eggs and milk in small bowl until frothy. Blend into flour mixture. Melt shortening with chocolate in small saucepan over low heat. Add to flour mixture and blend well. Spoon into prepared pan, spreading evenly. Bake until loaf is brown and toothpick inserted in center comes out clean, about 50 minutes. Serve bread warm.

Fresh Apple-Nut Bread

Makes one 9 × 5-inch loaf

¼ cup (½ stick) butter, room temperature
1 cup firmly packed light brown sugar
2 eggs
3 cups all purpose flour
2 cups grated peeled apple (about 2 large)

¾ cup chopped nuts
1½ teaspoons baking soda
1 teaspoon baking powder
1 teaspoon grated lemon peel
1 teaspoon salt
1 teaspoon cinnamon
¼ teaspoon freshly grated nutmeg
¾ cup buttermilk

Preheat oven to 350°F. Grease and flour 9 × 5-inch loaf pan. Cream butter and sugar in medium bowl. Beat in eggs. Combine next 9 ingredients in separate bowl and blend into creamed mixture alternately with buttermilk. Turn into pan and bake until toothpick inserted in center comes out clean, about 1 hour. Cool 10 minutes. Remove from pan and cool completely on wire rack.

Simple Banana Bread

Makes one 9 × 5-inch loaf

½ cup (1 stick) unsalted butter or margarine
1 cup sugar
2 eggs
1 cup mashed banana (about 2 large)
1 teaspoon fresh lemon juice

½ teaspoon banana extract
2 cups sifted all purpose flour
½ teaspoon baking soda
½ teaspoon baking powder
Pinch of salt
1½ tablespoons sour cream
½ cup chopped walnuts

Preheat oven to 350°F. Cream butter with sugar in large bowl. Beat in eggs. Blend in banana, lemon juice and banana extract. Resift flour with baking soda, baking powder and salt. Gradually add dry ingredients to creamed mixture alternately with sour cream, beating well after each addition. Stir in nuts. Turn into 9 × 5-inch loaf pan. Bake until tester inserted in center comes out clean, about 45 to 50 minutes. Let cool completely before slicing.

Best-Ever Banana Bread

Makes one 9 × 5-inch loaf

1¾ cups all purpose flour
1½ cups sugar
  1 cup chopped walnuts
  2 ripe medium bananas, mashed
  2 eggs

½ cup vegetable oil
¼ cup plus 1 tablespoon buttermilk
  1 teaspoon baking soda
  1 teaspoon vanilla
½ teaspoon salt

Preheat oven to 325°F. Grease and flour 9 × 5-inch loaf pan. Combine all ingredients in large bowl and mix well. Transfer to prepared pan. Bake until top is golden brown and splits slightly, about 1 hour and 20 minutes. Serve warm. *Do not double recipe.*

Blueberry Quick Bread

Makes 1 bundt cake, two 9 × 5-inch loaves or four 5⅝ × 3⅛-inch loaves

5 cups all purpose flour
1½ cups sugar
  2 tablespoons baking powder
  1 teaspoon cinnamon
  1 teaspoon salt
¾ cup (1½ sticks) butter or margarine
1½ cups chopped walnuts
  1 teaspoon grated lemon peel

4 eggs
2 cups milk
2 teaspoons vanilla
  Juice of 1 lemon
3 cups fresh or frozen blueberries*

Preheat oven to 350°F. Grease and flour 10-inch bundt or other pans. Combine flour, sugar, baking powder, cinnamon and salt in large bowl. Cut in butter until mixture resembles fine crumbs. Stir in walnuts and lemon peel.

Beat eggs lightly with fork in small bowl. Stir in milk, vanilla and lemon juice and mix well. Blend into flour mixture just until moistened. Gently stir in blueberries. Spoon evenly into pan(s) and bake until toothpick inserted in center comes out clean, about 80 to 90 minutes. Cool on wire rack 10 minutes. Remove from pan. Serve warm or at room temperature. Wrap and store in refrigerator.

*If blueberries are frozen, do not thaw.

Coconut Bread

Makes one 9 × 5-inch loaf

2¾ cups all purpose flour
  1 cup sugar
  1 tablespoon plus 1 teaspoon baking powder
  1 teaspoon salt
1¼ cups shredded coconut, toasted and cooled

1½ cups milk
  1 egg, lightly beaten
  2 tablespoons peanut oil
  1 teaspoon coconut extract

Preheat oven to 350°F. Lightly coat 9 × 5-inch loaf pan with vegetable spray. Sift flour, sugar, baking powder and salt into medium bowl. Add coconut and blend well.

Combine milk, egg, oil and extract in another bowl and mix well. Add to dry ingredients all at once, stirring briefly until just blended; *do not overmix.*

Turn batter into prepared pan. Bake until tester inserted in center of loaf comes out clean, about 1 hour. Let cool in pan 8 to 10 minutes. Invert onto wire rack and let cool to room temperature before slicing.

Clockwise from upper left: Finnish Cardamom Wreath with Whipped Spiced Butter; Slovenian Christmas Bread; St. Lucia Candle Crown and Lucia Buns; Norwegian Christmas Bread; Three Kings Bread; Danish Cinnamon Marzipan Kringle

Brian Leatart

Mexican Alligator Bread

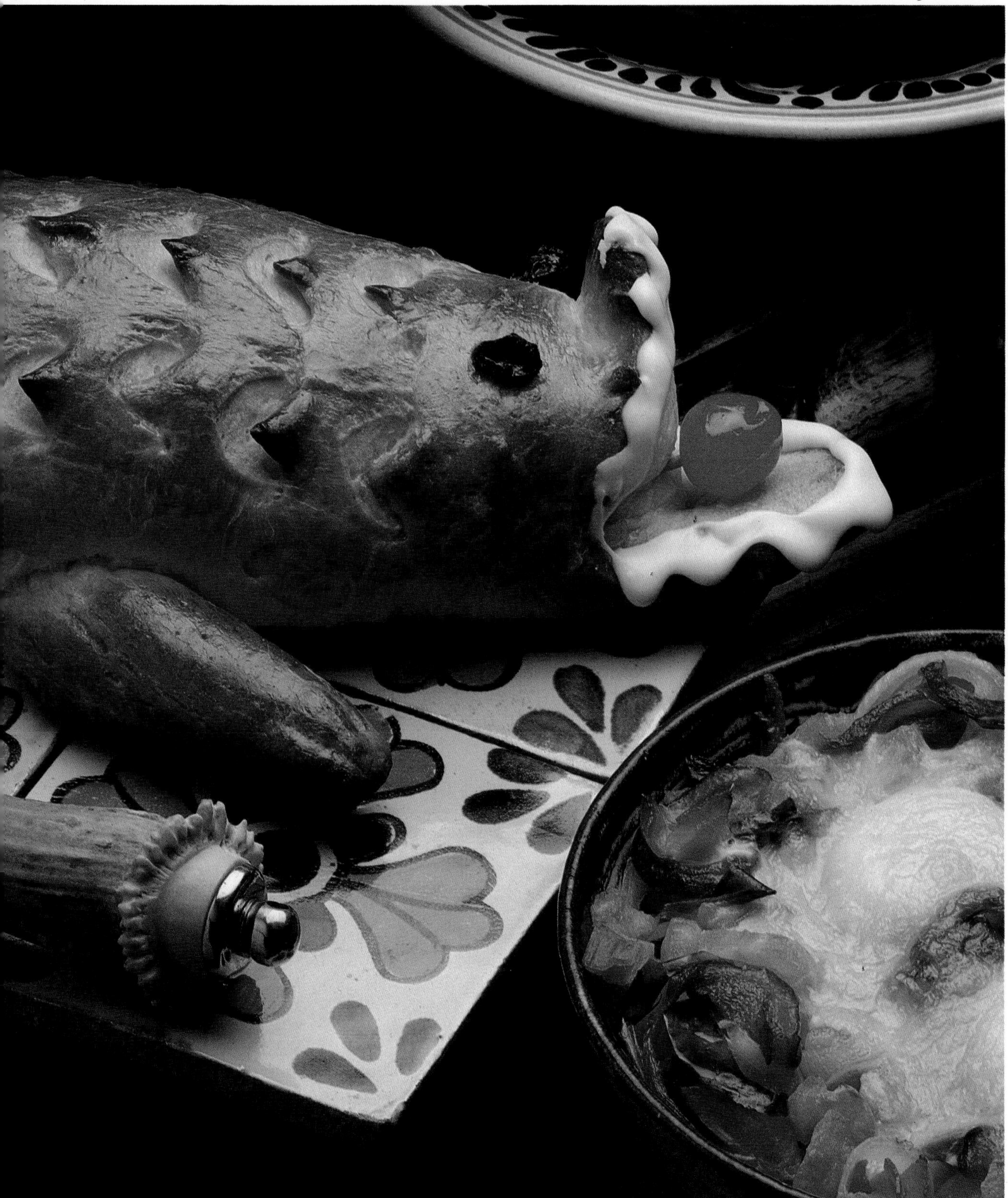

Christopsomo; Pangiallo; Spanish King's Bread; Czechoslovakian Vanocka. Center: Panpepato

Clockwise from upper right:
Cinnamon Grahams; Oatmeal
Hardtack; Scottish Currant
Shortbread; Chippewa Indian
Fried Bread; Graham Flatbrød
Cigars; Norwegian Potato
Lefse. Center: Indian Chapati

Alan Krosnick

Victor Scocozza

Cranberry Nut Bread

Makes one 9 × 5-inch loaf

2 cups sifted all purpose flour
1 cup sugar
1½ teaspoons baking powder
1 teaspoon salt
½ teaspoon baking soda
¼ cup solid vegetable shortening
¾ cup fresh orange juice

1 egg, well beaten
1 teaspoon grated orange peel
1 cup fresh or frozen cranberries,
 coarsely chopped, or 1 cup
 well-drained canned whole
 cranberries, coarsely chopped
½ cup chopped walnuts or pecans

Preheat oven to 350°F. Grease and flour 9 × 5-inch loaf pan. Sift dry ingredients into large bowl. Cut in shortening. Combine orange juice, egg and grated peel and add to dry ingredients, mixing just to moisten. Fold in berries and nuts. Turn into prepared pan and bake until tester inserted in center comes out clean, about 1 hour. Cool on wire rack before removing from pan. Wrap and store overnight to develop flavors before slicing.

Marsala Date Nut Bread

Makes one 9 × 5-inch loaf

2 eggs
2 cups all purpose flour
1 cup sugar
½ cup Marsala
¼ cup vegetable oil
1 tablespoon baking powder

¾ teaspoon salt
½ teaspoon baking soda
1½ cups coarsely chopped dates
1 cup coarsely chopped walnuts

Preheat oven to 350°F. Generously grease 9 × 5-inch loaf pan. Beat eggs in large bowl of electric mixer about 30 seconds at medium speed. Add remaining ingredients except dates and nuts and blend. Stir in dates and nuts. Turn into prepared pan and bake until tester inserted in center comes out clean, about 55 to 60 minutes. Remove from pan and let cool completely on rack.

Spirited Fruit Bread

Makes one 9 × 5-inch loaf

1 cup sugar
¾ cup (1½ sticks) butter, melted
 and cooled
2 eggs
2 tablespoons apricot brandy
2 tablespoons amaretto
2 teaspoons vanilla
1 cup mashed ripe banana
 (about 2 medium-large)
2 teaspoons pumpkin pie spice

2 teaspoons cinnamon
1 teaspoon baking soda
1 teaspoon baking powder
½ teaspoon salt

2 cups unbleached all purpose flour
1 6-ounce package dried apricots,
 finely chopped
1 cup (4 ounces) chopped walnuts

Preheat oven to 350°F. Grease and lightly flour 9 × 5-inch loaf pan. Combine sugar, melted butter, eggs, apricot brandy, amaretto and vanilla in large bowl and whisk until well blended, about 2 to 3 minutes. Stir in mashed banana. Combine pumpkin pie spice, cinnamon, baking soda, baking powder and salt in small bowl and mix well, making sure no lumps remain.

Whisk into banana mixture, blending well. Fold in flour using spatula; batter will be thick. Stir in chopped apricots and walnuts. Spoon batter into prepared pan. Bake until tester inserted in center comes out clean, about 50 to 55 minutes (top will split).

Let bread cool in pan 15 minutes. Remove from pan and cool completely on rack, about 2 to 3 hours. Wrap tightly in aluminum foil and store at room temperature for at least 2 days before serving.

Lemon Tea Loaf

Makes one 12-inch loaf

½ cup (1 stick) butter, room temperature
1 cup sugar
2 eggs, room temperature
1½ cups all purpose flour
1½ teaspoons baking powder
½ teaspoon salt
½ cup milk
½ cup chopped walnuts
3 tablespoons finely grated lemon peel (yellow and white parts)

Preheat oven to 350°F. Butter and flour 12 × 3½ × 2-inch loaf pan.* Cream butter with sugar in large bowl of electric mixer. Beat in eggs one at a time. Sift in flour, baking powder and salt and beat at low speed until smooth. Blend in milk. Fold in walnuts and lemon peel. Pour batter into prepared pan. Bake until tester inserted in center comes out clean, about 40 minutes. Cool in pan on rack 10 minutes. Invert loaf onto rack and cool completely before slicing.

*If unavailable, an 8 × 4-inch pan can be substituted. Bake for 1 hour.

Pineapple-Zucchini Loaf

Makes two 9 × 5-inch loaves

3 eggs
2 cups sugar
1 cup vegetable oil
3 tablespoons vanilla
2 cups peeled, grated and well-drained zucchini
3 cups all purpose flour
1 teaspoon baking powder
1 teaspoon baking soda
1 teaspoon salt
1 8-ounce can crushed pineapple, undrained
1 cup chopped pecans or walnuts
½ cup raisins (optional)

Preheat oven to 350°F. Grease and flour two 9 × 5-inch loaf pans. Beat eggs until fluffy. Add sugar, oil and vanilla and blend well. Add zucchini. Sift together flour, baking powder, soda and salt and add to batter. Stir in pineapple, nuts and raisins and mix well. Turn into pans and bake until tester inserted in center comes out clean, about 1 hour. Cool on wire rack before removing from pans. Wrap and store overnight to develop flavors before slicing.

Poppy Seed Bread

Makes two 9 × 5-inch loaves

3 eggs
1¼ cups evaporated milk
⅔ cup vegetable oil
1 teaspoon vanilla
2¼ cups sifted all purpose flour
1½ cups sugar
¾ cup poppy seeds
4½ teaspoons baking powder

Preheat oven to 350°F.* Grease and flour two 9 × 5-inch loaf pans. Lightly beat eggs in large mixing bowl. Add milk, oil and vanilla and beat well. Add dry ingredients and beat until smooth. Turn into pans and bake until tester inserted in center comes out clean, 45 to 50 minutes. Cool bread in pans 10 minutes, then turn out onto racks to cool completely.

*If using glass loaf pans bake at 325°F.

Whole Wheat Prune Loaf

Makes one 9 × 5-inch loaf

1¼ cups all purpose flour
1 teaspoon baking powder
1 teaspoon baking soda
½ teaspoon salt
¾ cup pitted prunes, cut into small pieces

⅓ cup molasses
⅓ cup firmly packed dark brown sugar

¼ cup vegetable oil
1½ cups sour milk*
1¼ cups stone-ground whole wheat flour
¾ cup chopped walnuts
Orange Cream Cheese**

Preheat oven to 375°F. Generously grease 9 × 5-inch loaf pan. Line bottom and sides of pan with waxed paper.

Sift all purpose flour, baking powder, baking soda and salt into medium bowl. Spread prunes on sheet of waxed paper. Sprinkle prunes evenly with 1 tablespoon flour mixture.

Combine molasses, sugar and oil in large bowl of electric mixer and beat at medium speed until well blended. Add flour mixture, sour milk and whole wheat flour alternately to molasses mixture, stirring well with wooden spoon after each addition. Stir in prunes and nuts. Transfer batter to prepared pan. Bake until tester inserted in center comes out clean, about 55 minutes. Let cool in pan on rack 10 minutes. Remove loaf from pan and discard waxed paper. Let cool completely on rack. Serve with orange cream cheese.

*For sour milk, place 2 tablespoons fresh lemon juice in measuring cup. Add enough milk to equal 1½ cups liquid. Stir gently.

**Orange Cream Cheese

6 ounces cream cheese, room temperature
3 tablespoons sugar

3 tablespoons whipping cream
1½ teaspoons grated orange peel

Mix all ingredients until creamy.

Pumpkin-Apple Bundt Bread

8 to 10 servings

2 cups unbleached all purpose flour
1 tablespoon baking powder
½ teaspoon baking soda
½ teaspoon salt
½ teaspoon cinnamon
½ teaspoon freshly grated nutmeg
¼ teaspoon ground cloves
¼ teaspoon ground ginger
1½ cups sugar
2 eggs

½ cup plus 2 tablespoons (1¼ sticks) unsalted butter (room temperature), cut into 5 pieces
1 cup canned pumpkin
2 cups (about 2 large) loosely packed, unpeeled shredded tart apples (Granny Smith or greening)
2 tablespoons powdered sugar (optional)

Position rack in center of oven and preheat to 350°F. Generously butter 12-cup bundt pan; set aside.

If using food processor, mix first 8 ingredients; remove from work bowl and set aside. Process sugar and eggs until fluffy. Add butter and process 1 minute. Add pumpkin and apples and process 2 seconds. Add dry ingredients, combining with as few on/off turns as possible to just blend flour into batter; *do not overprocess or texture will be coarse.*

If using mixer, combine first 8 ingredients and blend well; set aside. Cream butter and sugar in large mixing bowl. Add eggs and pumpkin and mix until fluffy. Add apples and blend thoroughly. Mix in dry ingredients.

Turn batter into prepared pan and bake until bread begins to pull away from sides of pan, about 50 to 55 minutes. Remove from oven and let stand on wire rack 5 minutes. Invert onto rack and cool completely. Sift powdered sugar onto bread just before serving, if desired.

This bread freezes very well.

Wine Country Inn's Pumpkin Raisin Bread

Makes two 9 × 5-inch loaves

2/3 cup butter or solid vegetable shortening
2²/3 cups sugar
4 eggs
1 1-pound can pumpkin
2/3 cup water
2½ cups all purpose flour
1 cup whole wheat flour

2 teaspoons baking soda
1½ teaspoons salt
1 teaspoon ground cloves
1 teaspoon cinnamon
½ teaspoon cardamom
½ teaspoon baking powder
1½ cups raisins

Preheat oven to 350°F. Generously grease two 9 × 5-inch loaf pans. Cream butter or shortening with sugar in large mixing bowl until light and fluffy. Beat in eggs until well blended. Stir in pumpkin and water, mixing well. Sift flours, baking soda, salt, spices and baking powder into large bowl. Stir into pumpkin, mixing just until blended. Add raisins. Divide batter evenly between prepared pans. Bake until loaves are browned and tester inserted in center comes out clean, about 1¼ hours. Let loaves cool completely in pans before serving.

Rhubarb Nut Bread

Makes two 9 × 5-inch loaves or four 5⁵/8 × 3¹/8-inch loaves

1½ cups firmly packed brown sugar
3/4 cup vegetable oil
1 egg
2½ cups unsifted all purpose flour
1 cup sour milk or 15 tablespoons milk mixed with 1 tablespoon white vinegar
1 teaspoon salt

1 teaspoon baking soda
1 teaspoon cinnamon
1 teaspoon vanilla
2½ cups chopped fresh or unsweetened frozen rhubarb*
½ cup chopped walnuts or pecans
½ cup sugar
1 tablespoon butter

Preheat oven to 325°F. Generously grease and flour loaf pans. Using electric mixer, beat brown sugar, oil and egg in large bowl. Add next 6 ingredients and mix on low speed. Fold in rhubarb and nuts. Turn into pans, spreading evenly. Thoroughly blend sugar and butter and sprinkle evenly over batter. Bake until toothpick inserted in center comes out clean, about 1 hour; *do not overbake.* Cool on wire rack before removing from pans. Wrap and store overnight to develop flavors.

*If rhubarb is frozen, do not thaw.

Betty's Zucchini Bread

Makes 1 bundt cake or two 8 × 4-inch loaves

2 cups all purpose flour
2 to 3 teaspoons cinnamon
2 teaspoons baking soda
1 teaspoon salt
½ teaspoon baking powder
3 eggs

2 cups sugar
¾ cup vegetable oil
2 cups well drained grated zucchini
1½ cups chopped walnuts
½ cup raisins (optional)

Preheat oven to 350°F. Grease and flour 12-cup bundt pan or two 8 × 4-inch loaf pans. Sift first 5 ingredients. Beat eggs in large bowl until light. Gradually add sugar and beat until thick and lemon colored. Add oil in thin stream and beat well. Mix in zucchini, nuts and raisins. Add sifted dry ingredients and blend well. Turn into prepared pan(s). Bake until tester inserted in center comes out clean, about 50 minutes. Let cool 5 minutes before turning out onto rack. Cool completely before slicing.

Zucchini Date Nut Loaf

Makes one 9 × 5-inch loaf

1¾ cups all purpose flour
¾ teaspoon baking powder
¾ teaspoon cinnamon
½ teaspoon baking soda
½ teaspoon cardamom
¼ teaspoon allspice
¼ teaspoon salt
¾ cup dates, cut into small pieces

1 cup sugar
2 eggs
½ cup vegetable oil
1 cup grated unpeeled zucchini
¾ cup chopped walnuts

Preheat oven to 350°F. Generously grease 9 × 5-inch loaf pan. Line bottom and sides with waxed paper.

Sift flour, baking powder, cinnamon, baking soda, cardamom, allspice and salt into medium bowl. Spread dates on sheet of waxed paper. Sprinkle with 1 tablespoon flour mixture.

Combine sugar, eggs and oil in large bowl of electric mixer and beat at medium speed until well blended. Add flour mixture and zucchini alternately to egg mixture, stirring well with wooden spoon after each addition. Stir in dates and nuts. Transfer batter to prepared pan. Bake until tester inserted in center comes out clean, about 70 to 75 minutes. Let cool in pan on rack 10 minutes. Remove loaf from pan and discard waxed paper. Let cool completely on rack before serving.

Strawberry Bread

Makes one 9 × 5-inch loaf

1 10-ounce package frozen strawberries packed in syrup, thawed (undrained)
¾ cup vegetable oil
2 eggs

1½ cups all purpose flour
1 cup sugar
1 teaspoon cinnamon
½ teaspoon baking soda

Preheat oven to 325°F. Lightly grease 9 × 5-inch loaf pan. Puree strawberries in blender or processor. Combine oil and eggs in small bowl and whisk thoroughly. Sift remaining ingredients into large bowl. Make well in center. Pour in eggs and puree and stir with wooden spoon just until blended. Pour into prepared pan. Bake until tester inserted in center comes out clean, about 1 hour and 10 minutes. Let cool completely on rack.

Oatmeal Buttermilk Loaf

Makes one 8½ × 4½-inch loaf

1½ cups all purpose flour
1 teaspoon baking soda
¾ teaspoon baking powder
¼ teaspoon salt
½ cup sugar
⅓ cup honey

¼ cup (½ stick) butter, melted
1 egg
1 cup buttermilk
¾ cup rolled oats
½ cup raisins

Preheat oven to 350°F. Generously grease 8½ × 4½-inch loaf pan. Line bottom and sides with waxed paper.

Sift flour, baking soda, baking powder and salt into medium bowl and set aside. Combine sugar, honey, butter and egg in large bowl of electric mixer and beat at medium speed until light and fluffy. Reduce speed to low. Add flour mixture, buttermilk and oats alternately to egg mixture, beating well after each addition. Stir in raisins. Transfer batter to prepared pan, smoothing top. Bake until tester inserted in center comes out clean, about 55 to 60 minutes. Let cool in pan on rack 10 minutes. Remove loaf from pan and discard waxed paper. Let cool completely on rack before serving.

Buttermilk Pecan Bread

Makes two 8 × 4-inch loaves

2 eggs
½ cup firmly packed brown sugar
½ cup honey
1 teaspoon vanilla
3⅓ cups whole wheat pastry flour
2 teaspoons baking powder

½ teaspoon baking soda
½ teaspoon salt
½ teaspoon ground cardamom
2 cups buttermilk
1 cup chopped pecans

Grease two 8 × 4-inch loaf pans. Beat eggs with sugar, honey and vanilla. Sift dry ingredients and add to egg mixture alternately with buttermilk, beginning and ending with dry ingredients and blending well after each addition. Stir in nuts. Divide between pans and let stand at room temperature 25 to 30 minutes to allow acidity to develop for rising.

Preheat oven to 325°F. Bake loaves until tester inserted in center comes out clean, about 1 hour. Let cool in pans on rack 10 minutes, then turn out onto rack to cool completely.

Easy Raisin Bread

Makes one 9 × 5-inch loaf

1 cup raisins
1 teaspoon baking soda
1 cup boiling water

1½ cups all purpose flour
½ cup sugar

½ teaspoon salt
1 egg, beaten to blend
1 tablespoon vegetable oil
Butter or cream cheese

Combine raisins and baking soda in small bowl. Add 1 cup boiling water. Cool 30 minutes.

Preheat oven to 350°F. Grease and flour 9 × 5-inch loaf pan. Mix flour, sugar and salt in medium bowl. Stir in raisin mixture, egg and oil. Pour into prepared pan. Bake until golden brown and tester inserted in center comes out clean, about 45 minutes. Cool 10 minutes in pan. Serve raisin bread warm with butter or cream cheese.

Molasses-Caraway Quick Bread

Makes one 8½ × 4½-inch loaf

2¼ cups all purpose flour
1 cup milk, room temperature
½ cup sugar
¼ cup molasses

¼ cup golden raisins
1 tablespoon baking powder
1 teaspoon caraway seeds
½ teaspoon salt

Grease 8½ × 4½-inch loaf pan. Combine all ingredients in large bowl of electric mixer and blend well. Spoon batter into prepared pan. Let stand in warm draft-free area 25 minutes.

Preheat oven to 350°F. Bake bread until tester inserted in center comes out clean, about 35 minutes. Cool in pan on rack 10 minutes. Turn out onto rack and cool completely.

Irish Stout Loaf

Makes one 8½ × 4½-inch loaf

2 cups sifted all purpose flour
1 teaspoon cream of tartar
¼ teaspoon baking soda
¼ teaspoon salt
1 cup raisins
1 cup diced mixed glacéed fruit

½ cup (1 stick) butter, room temperature
1 teaspoon cinnamon

1 teaspoon ground ginger
½ teaspoon freshly grated nutmeg
¼ teaspoon ground cloves
¾ cup sugar
⅔ cup firmly packed dark brown sugar
¼ cup sour cream
1 egg
½ cup flat stout

Preheat oven to 350°F. Generously grease 8½ × 4½-inch loaf pan. Line bottom and sides with waxed paper.

Resift flour with cream of tartar, baking soda and salt into medium bowl and set aside. Spread raisins and glacéed fruit on sheet of waxed paper. Sprinkle with 2 tablespoons flour mixture (use fingertips to separate pieces of fruit for even coating).

Combine butter, cinnamon, ginger, nutmeg and cloves in large bowl of electric mixer and beat at medium speed until well blended. Add sugars, sour cream and egg and blend well. Reduce speed to low. Add flour mixture and stout alternately to egg mixture, beating well after each addition. Stir in raisins and mixed fruit. Transfer batter to prepared pan, smoothing top. Bake until tester inserted in center comes out clean, about 1½ hours. Let cool in pan on rack 10 minutes. Remove loaf from pan and discard waxed paper. Let cool completely on rack. Wrap airtight and let stand at least 24 hours before serving.

Applesauce Nut Bread

Makes one 9 × 5-inch loaf

1½ cups whole wheat pastry flour
1½ teaspoons cinnamon
1 teaspoon baking powder
1 teaspoon baking soda
1 teaspoon salt
½ teaspoon freshly grated nutmeg
⅓ cup butter or margarine, room temperature

½ cup firmly packed dark brown sugar
1½ cups smooth, thick applesauce
2 eggs
1 cup quick-cooking rolled oats
1 cup chopped walnuts
½ cup raisins (plumped, if desired)

Preheat oven to 350°F. Lightly grease 9 × 5-inch loaf pan. Sift together first 6 ingredients; set aside. Cream butter and sugar in large mixing bowl. Thoroughly beat in applesauce and eggs. Add sifted dry ingredients and blend well. Stir in oats, nuts and raisins. Turn into prepared pan. Bake until bread is golden brown and tester inserted in center comes out clean, about 55 to 60 minutes. Cool slightly in pan, then remove and let cool completely on rack.

Lemon-Apple Bread

Makes two 8 × 4-inch loaves

2 cups unbleached all purpose flour
1 tablespoon baking powder
1 teaspoon baking soda
1 teaspoon salt
1 teaspoon cinnamon
¼ teaspoon freshly grated nutmeg
½ cup walnuts or pecans (2 ounces)

2 large tart apples (12 ounces total), preferably Granny Smith, peeled, cored and quartered
Peel of 1 large lemon

1⅓ cups sugar
3 eggs
½ cup (1 stick) unsalted butter, room temperature, cut into 4 pieces
1 tablespoon fresh lemon juice
1 teaspoon vanilla

Butter two 8 × 4-inch loaf pans (5 cups each). Dust lightly with flour, shaking off excess. Position rack in center of oven and preheat to 350°F.

Insert steel knife into processor. Combine flour, baking powder, baking soda, salt, cinnamon, nutmeg and nuts in work bowl and mix 10 seconds. Set aside.

Combine apples and lemon peel in work bowl and chop coarsely using 3 on/off turns, then puree, stopping machine as necessary to scrape down sides of bowl. (Puree should measure 1⅔ cups.) Add sugar and eggs and blend 1 minute. Add butter, lemon juice and vanilla and mix 1 minute longer. Add dry ingredients and blend using on/off turns; *do not overmix*.

Spoon batter into prepared pans, spreading evenly. Bake until loaves are browned, about 40 to 45 minutes. Cool in pans 10 minutes. Turn out onto rack and let cool completely.

Rhubarb Bread

Makes two 9 × 5-inch loaves

1½ cups firmly packed brown sugar
⅔ cup vegetable oil
1 cup buttermilk
1 egg
1 teaspoon vanilla
1 teaspoon baking soda
1 teaspoon salt
2½ cups all purpose flour

1½ cups chopped uncooked fresh rhubarb
½ cup chopped nuts

½ cup sugar
1½ tablespoons grated orange peel
1 tablespoon butter, room temperature

Preheat oven to 350°F. Grease two 9 × 5-inch loaf pans; line bottom and sides with waxed paper. Combine brown sugar and oil in large bowl and beat well. Mix buttermilk, egg, vanilla, baking soda and salt in small bowl. Add to brown sugar mixture and blend thoroughly. Gently fold in flour, rhubarb and nuts. Divide batter evenly between prepared loaf pans.

Combine sugar, orange peel and butter in small bowl and blend well with fork. Sprinkle over batter. Bake until tester inserted in center of loaves comes out clean, about 1 hour. Let cool in pans 10 minutes, then turn out onto racks. Remove waxed paper when loaves are completely cool.

Apricot-Prune Batter Bread

Served with Continental breakfast at the Greenwood Lodge, an inn in Elk, California.

Makes one 10-inch round loaf

¾ cup dried apricots (4 ounces)
¾ cup pitted prunes (5½ ounces)
1 tablespoon all purpose flour

½ cup firmly packed light brown sugar
2 tablespoons (¼ stick) butter, room temperature
2 tablespoons all purpose flour
1 teaspoon cinnamon

3 cups all purpose flour
1½ teaspoons baking powder

¾ teaspoon baking soda
¼ teaspoon salt
¾ cup (1½ sticks) butter, room temperature
1½ cups sugar
4 eggs
1½ teaspoons vanilla
1 cup sour cream

Powdered sugar

Preheat oven to 350°F. Butter and lightly flour 10-inch tube pan, shaking out excess. Coarsely chop apricots and prunes. Transfer to small bowl. Add 1 tablespoon flour and toss lightly to blend.

Combine brown sugar, 2 tablespoons butter, 2 tablespoons flour and cinnamon in bowl and mix with fork until crumbly.

Sift 3 cups flour, baking powder, baking soda and salt onto sheet of waxed paper. Cream ¾ cup butter in large bowl of electric mixer until fluffy, about 1 minute. Gradually beat in sugar, stopping once to scrape down sides of bowl. Add eggs one at a time, beating well after each addition. Continue beating until mixture is light and fluffy, about 3 minutes. Mix in vanilla. Add ¼ of flour mixture and beat at low speed. Add ⅓ cup sour cream. Repeat, adding flour mixture alternately with sour cream, ending with flour. Beat just until smooth, about 1 minute. Fold in apricots and prunes and mix well using spatula. Spoon ⅓ of batter into prepared pan, spreading evenly. Crumble ⅓ of brown sugar mixture atop batter. Repeat with remaining batter and brown sugar mixture. Bake until tester inserted in center comes out clean, about 1 hour and 15 minutes.

Let cool slightly. Turn out onto rack. Dust with powdered sugar. Serve warm.

Prune Bread

Makes two 8 × 4-inch loaves

2½ cups unbleached all purpose flour
1 teaspoon baking soda
1 teaspoon baking powder
1 teaspoon cream of tartar
1 teaspoon salt

28 pitted prunes
½ cup boiling water
1¼ cups sugar
3 eggs

¼ cup vegetable oil
¾ cup plus 1 tablespoon fresh orange juice
3 tablespoons fresh lemon juice
1 teaspoon vanilla

Butter two 8 × 4-inch bread pans (5 cups each). Dust lightly with flour, shaking off excess. Position rack in center of oven and preheat to 350°F.

Insert steel knife into processor. Combine flour, baking soda, baking powder, cream of tartar and salt in work bowl and blend 10 seconds. Set aside.

Chop prunes in processor 10 seconds. Add boiling water and mix 5 seconds longer. Add sugar and eggs and blend 1 minute. Add oil and mix 1 minute. Add citrus juices and vanilla and process 5 seconds. Add dry ingredients and blend 30ing on/off turns just until flour is incorporated, stopping once to scrape sides of work bowl; *do not overmix.*

Divide dough evenly between prepared pans. Bake until loaves are well browned, about 60 to 65 minutes. Cool in pans 10 minutes. Turn out onto rack and let cool completely.

Light Bran Muffins

The batter for these light, sweet muffins can be stored in the refrigerator for several days.

Makes about 28

1 cup boiling water
1 cup 100% Bran cereal
9 tablespoons magarine, room temperature

2 eggs
1 cup sugar

2 cups buttermilk
2½ cups all purpose flour
2 cups All-Bran cereal
2½ teaspoons baking soda

Pour boiling water over 100% Bran cereal and margarine in bowl. Stir until margarine is melted. Cool to room temperature.

Using electric mixer, beat eggs and sugar in medium bowl until thoroughly blended. Mix in buttermilk. Add to cooled bran mixture and beat well. Combine flour, All-Bran cereal and baking soda in another large bowl. Add to buttermilk mixture and stir just until flour is moistened. Cover with plastic and refrigerate at least 2 hours.

Preheat oven to 400°F. Generously grease muffin cups. Spoon batter into prepared cups, filling ¾ full. Bake until lightly browned and tester inserted in centers comes out clean, about 20 minutes. Serve muffins warm or at room temperature.

Peanut Butter-Bran Muffins

Makes about 3 dozen

2 cups bran cereal
1 cup boiling water
1 cup golden raisins
½ cup rolled oats
½ cup wheat germ
2 cups plain yogurt or buttermilk
⅔ cup honey
2 eggs
⅓ cup molasses

⅓ cup chunky peanut butter
2 tablespoons safflower oil
1 cup whole wheat pastry flour, sifted
1 cup all purpose flour, sifted
½ cup soya flour, sifted
2½ teaspoons baking soda
½ teaspoon salt

Preheat oven to 375°F. Place paper liners in muffin tins. Combine bran, boiling water, raisins, oats and wheat germ in medium bowl and let soften several minutes. Mix yogurt or buttermilk, honey, eggs, molasses, peanut butter and oil in large bowl. Stir in bran mixture. Blend dry ingredients into batter. Fill liners ¾ full. Bake muffins until golden, about 25 minutes. Serve warm or at room temperature.
These muffins freeze well.

Sour Cream Orange Muffins

These muffins do not rise into the usual rounded tops, but they are delectable. For best results bake only in very small muffin cups.

Makes 3 dozen mini-muffins

6 tablespoons (¾ stick) butter, cut into pieces
1½ cups sugar
1 egg
½ cup sour cream
½ teaspoon orange extract

1¼ cups all purpose flour
½ teaspoon baking soda

½ teaspoon salt
½ cup chopped pecans
3 tablespoons grated orange peel
2 tablespoons plus 2 teaspoons fresh orange juice

Preheat oven to 375°F. Coat mini-muffin pan with vegetable spray. Cream butter with sugar in medium bowl. Beat in egg. Stir in sour cream and orange extract.
Sift flour, baking soda and salt. Blend into batter. Add pecans, orange peel and juice and mix well. Spoon into prepared pan, filling each cup ¾ full. Bake until tester inserted in centers of muffins comes out clean, about 18 minutes. Serve warm.

Orange-Pecan Muffins

Makes 12

½ cup sugar
½ cup fresh orange juice
1 egg, beaten to blend
2 tablespoons vegetable oil
2 cups biscuit mix
½ cup orange marmalade
½ cup chopped pecans

Topping
¼ cup sugar
1½ tablespoons all purpose flour
½ teaspoon cinnamon
½ teaspoon freshly grated nutmeg
1 tablespoon butter

Preheat oven to 400°F. Generously grease muffin tin or line with paper cups. Combine sugar, orange juice, egg and oil in medium bowl and blend well. Add biscuit mix and beat vigorously 30 seconds. Stir in marmalade and pecans. Turn into muffin tin, filling each cup ⅔ full.
For topping: Combine sugar, flour, cinnamon and nutmeg in small bowl. Cut in butter until mixture is crumbly. Sprinkle over batter and bake 20 to 25 minutes. Serve muffins warm or at room temperature.

Banana Muffins

Makes 15

3 large ripe bananas
1 cup sugar
1 egg, beaten to blend
1½ cups all purpose flour
1 teaspoon baking soda
1 teaspoon baking powder

¾ teaspoon salt
⅓ cup vegetable oil
½ cup chopped walnuts
Butter

Preheat oven to 375°F. Grease fifteen 2½-inch muffin cups. Mash bananas in large bowl. Mix in sugar and egg. Sift flour, baking soda, baking powder and salt. Add to banana mixture in 3 batches alternately with oil. Stir in walnuts. Fill prepared muffin cups ⅔ full. Bake until muffins are golden and tester inserted in centers comes out clean, 25 to 30 minutes. Cool slightly in tins on rack. Serve warm with butter.

Buttermilk Apple Muffins

Rhubarb can be substituted for the apple in these muffins.

Makes 12

1 cup firmly packed brown sugar
⅓ cup vegetable oil
1 egg, beaten to blend
1 teaspoon vanilla
1½ cups unbleached all purpose flour
½ teaspoon baking soda

¼ teaspoon salt
1 cup chopped peeled apple
½ cup buttermilk
¼ cup walnuts, chopped
½ teaspoon cinnamon

Preheat oven to 325°F. Place paper liners in muffin tins. Blend ¾ cup brown sugar, oil, egg and vanilla in large bowl. Add flour, baking soda and salt. Add apple and buttermilk and mix thoroughly. Divide among lined muffin tins. Combine remaining ¼ cup brown sugar, walnuts and cinnamon in small bowl. Sprinkle over batter. Bake until muffins are browned and toothpick inserted in centers comes out clean, 30 to 35 minutes. Serve muffins warm.

Wheat-Raisin Muffins

Makes 12

1 cup milk
¼ cup honey or molasses
¼ cup safflower oil
1 egg
1⅓ cups all purpose flour
2 tablespoons sugar

2 teaspoons baking soda
½ teaspoon salt
½ teaspoon cinnamon
¼ teaspoon freshly grated nutmeg
2⅓ cups Wheatena
½ cup raisins

Preheat oven to 375°F. Grease muffin cups. Combine milk, honey or molasses, oil and egg in small bowl. Sift flour, sugar, baking soda, salt, cinnamon and nutmeg into medium bowl. Mix in Wheatena. Make well in center and pour in milk mixture, mixing just until blended. Stir in raisins. Fill muffin cups ¾ full. Bake until tester inserted in centers comes out clean, about 20 minutes. Serve warm or at room temperature.

Blueberry-Oatmeal Muffins

Makes 18

1 cup plus 2 tablespoons quick-cooking rolled oats
1 cup buttermilk
1 tablespoon vanilla

1 cup unbleached all purpose flour
1 tablespoon baking powder
1 teaspoon salt
1 teaspoon cinnamon

½ teaspoon baking soda
½ teaspoon freshly grated nutmeg
¼ cup walnuts (1 ounce)
¾ cup firmly packed light brown sugar
1 egg
¼ cup (½ stick) unsalted butter

1⅓ cups blueberries (7 ounces)

Generously butter 18 large muffin cups. Position rack in center of oven and preheat to 400°F.

Blend oats, buttermilk and vanilla in medium bowl and set aside.

Insert steel knife into processor. Combine flour, baking powder, salt, cinnamon, baking soda, nutmeg and walnuts in work bowl and mix until nuts are finely chopped, about 10 seconds. Remove and set aside. Combine brown sugar and egg in work bowl and blend 1 minute. Add butter and process 1 minute longer.

Add buttermilk mixture and process 2 seconds. Add dry ingredients and blend using on/off turns just until flour is incorporated; *do not overmix.* Transfer batter to large bowl. Fold in berries.

Fill muffin cups half full with batter. Bake until muffins are lightly browned, about 15 to 20 minutes. Turn out onto rack and let cool slightly.

Buttermilk-Bran Muffins

Makes 16

2 cups unprocessed bran flakes
1 cup all purpose flour
1 teaspoon baking soda
1 teaspoon salt
1¼ cups buttermilk

½ cup molasses
1 egg
¼ cup raisins
2 teaspoons honey

Preheat oven to 375°F. Place paper liners in muffin tins. Combine first 4 ingredients in large bowl. Stir in remaining ingredients, mixing thoroughly. Fill liners ¾ full. Bake until tester inserted in centers comes out clean, about 25 minutes. Serve warm.

Raisin Bran Muffins

Makes about 3 dozen

4 cups Raisin Bran cereal
2½ cups all purpose flour
1 cup sugar
2½ teaspoons baking soda

1½ teaspoons salt
2 cups buttermilk
2 eggs, beaten to blend
½ cup vegetable oil

Preheat oven to 400°F. Generously grease muffin cups. Combine cereal, flour, sugar, baking soda and salt in large bowl. Stir in buttermilk, eggs and oil and mix thoroughly. Spoon batter into prepared tins, filling cups ⅔ full. Bake until golden brown, about 20 minutes. Serve warm.

Zucchini Nut Muffins

Makes about 28

3 cups all purpose flour
1 teaspoon baking powder
1 teaspoon baking soda
1 teaspoon salt
1 teaspoon cinnamon
2 cups sugar
4 eggs, room temperature

1 cup oil (preferably soybean)
2 cups grated unpeeled zucchini (about 12 ounces)
1/2 teaspoon vanilla
1 cup chopped walnuts
1/2 cup golden raisins

Preheat oven to 350°F. Generously grease standard-size muffin pans. Sift flour, baking powder, baking soda, salt and cinnamon; set aside. Combine sugar and eggs in large bowl of electric mixer and beat at medium speed 2 minutes. Gradually add oil in slow, steady stream, beating constantly 2 to 3 minutes. Add zucchini and vanilla and blend well. Stir in walnuts and raisins. Fold in sifted dry ingredients just until batter is evenly moistened; *do not overmix.*

Spoon batter into prepared muffin pans, filling 2/3 full. Bake until lightly browned, about 25 minutes. Let stand 10 minutes, then turn muffins out onto racks to cool.

Zucchini Muffins

Makes 12 to 15

2 cups whole wheat flour
1 tablespoon baking powder
1 teaspoon cinnamon
3/4 teaspoon salt
3/4 cup milk
2 eggs

1/3 cup vegetable oil
1/4 cup honey
1 cup coarsely grated zucchini
2/3 cup raisins

Preheat oven to 375°F. Oil muffin cups. Sift or stir together dry ingredients. In small bowl, beat milk, eggs, oil and honey. Add to dry ingredients, stirring *just enough to moisten.* Quickly stir in zucchini and raisins and spoon into prepared muffin cups. Bake 20 to 25 minutes, or until golden brown.

Sugared Pumpkin Muffins

Makes 12

1 1/2 cups all purpose flour
1/2 cup sugar
2 teaspoons baking powder
1/2 teaspoon salt
1/2 teaspoon cinnamon
1/2 teaspoon freshly grated nutmeg

1/4 cup (1/2 stick) butter or margarine
1/2 cup milk
1/2 cup mashed cooked or canned pumpkin
1 egg
1 tablespoon sugar

Preheat oven to 400°F. Generously grease 12 muffin cups. Combine flour, 1/2 cup sugar, baking powder, salt, cinnamon and nutmeg in large bowl and mix well. Cut in butter until mixture resembles coarse meal. Stir in milk, pumpkin and egg, mixing thoroughly. Fill muffin cups 2/3 full. Sprinkle 1/4 teaspoon sugar over each. Bake until tester inserted in centers comes out clean, about 20 to 22 minutes. Loosen muffins from cups and cool on wire rack.

Becky's Blueberry-Buttermilk Biscuits

Makes about 12

2 cups sifted all purpose flour

1/2 cup sugar
1 tablespoon baking powder
1 teaspoon grated orange peel
1 teaspoon salt
1/4 teaspoon baking soda
1/3 cup solid vegetable shortening
3/4 cup buttermilk
1 egg, beaten to blend

1/2 cup frozen blueberries
(do not thaw)

3 tablespoons butter, melted
3 tablespoons sugar
1/4 teaspoon cinnamon
1/8 teaspoon freshly grated nutmeg

Preheat oven to 400°F. Lightly grease baking sheet. Combine first 6 ingredients in large bowl. Cut in shortening until mixture resembles coarse meal. Combine buttermilk and egg and mix into dry ingredients. Stir in blueberries. Gently knead on heavily floured surface until dough just holds together, 5 to 6 times. Pat out 1/2 inch thick. Cut with floured 3-inch cookie cutter or glass. Arrange on prepared sheet, spacing 2 inches apart. Bake until light brown, about 20 minutes.

Transfer biscuits to racks. Combine all remaining ingredients and brush over warm biscuits. Serve immediately.

Currant-Marsala Scones

Marsala adds a twist to this traditional scone. Perfect at tea time.

Makes 12

3/4 cup dried currants
1/3 cup sweet Marsala

1 1/2 cups sifted unbleached all purpose flour
1/2 cup whole wheat flour
1 tablespoon baking powder
1/4 teaspoon salt
1/3 cup firmly packed dark brown sugar

1 teaspoon grated lemon peel
6 tablespoons (3/4 stick) unsalted butter, chopped, room temperature
1 egg, beaten to blend
3/4 cup (about) half and half
Melted butter
Sugar

Combine currants and Marsala in heavy small saucepan and bring to boil, stirring constantly. Cover and let stand overnight, stirring occasionally.

Position rack in center of oven and preheat to 450°F. Sift flours, baking powder and salt into medium bowl. Add any large pieces of wheat caught in sifter. Mix in brown sugar and peel. Cut in butter until mixture resembles coarse meal. Drain currants; stir into mixture. Make well in center. Place egg in measuring cup. Blend in enough half and half to equal 3/4 cup. Add to well. Stir just until dough comes together. Turn out onto well-floured surface and knead gently just until dough holds together, about 12 times. Cut dough into 3 pieces. Gently pat each piece into 3/4-inch-thick round. Cut each round into quarters, pushing straight down with floured sharp knife. Arrange on ungreased baking sheet, spacing 1/2 inch apart. Brush tops with melted butter and sprinkle with sugar. Bake until light brown, about 14 minutes. Cool for 5 minutes on rack before serving.

Pumpkin Fritters

A specialty of Sandy Beach, a resort hotel on the south shore of Barbados.

8 servings

1 cup all purpose flour
½ cup sugar
1 teaspoon freshly grated nutmeg
½ teaspoon baking powder

1 cup water
1 1-pound can solid pack pumpkin
2 cups vegetable oil

Combine flour, sugar, nutmeg and baking powder in large bowl. Make well in center. Add water to well. Gradually draw flour mixture from inner edge of well into center until completely incorporated. Add pumpkin and mix thoroughly. Let batter stand at room temperature for 30 minutes.

Heat oil in deep fryer or heavy large skillet to 375°F. Drop batter into oil by teaspoons (do not crowd) and fry until brown, turning frequently, about 5 minutes. Drain on paper towels. Serve immediately.

Chocolate Chip Hearts

Makes about 10 biscuits

Boiling water
⅓ cup raisins

1¾ cups sifted unbleached all purpose flour
¼ cup whole wheat flour
6 tablespoons sugar
2½ teaspoons baking powder
½ teaspoon baking soda
½ teaspoon cinnamon
¼ teaspoon salt
½ cup (1 stick) unsalted butter, chopped, room temperature

3 ounces bittersweet or semisweet chocolate, cut into ¼-inch pieces
½ cup toasted pecans, coarsely chopped
2 eggs
¾ cup (about) buttermilk
½ teaspoon vanilla
Melted butter
Sugar

Pour boiling water over raisins to cover. Let soak 5 minutes. Drain; pat dry.

Position rack in center of oven and preheat to 450°F. Sift flours, 6 tablespoons sugar, baking powder, baking soda, cinnamon and salt into medium bowl. Add any large pieces of wheat caught in sifter. Cut in butter until mixture resembles coarse meal. Mix in raisins, chocolate and pecans. Make well in center. Place eggs in measuring cup. Blend in enough buttermilk to equal ¾ cup. Stir in vanilla. Add to well. Stir just until mixture is evenly moistened. Turn dough out onto well-floured surface and knead gently just until dough holds together, about 10 times. Roll out gently to thickness of 1 inch. Cut out hearts using 2½- to 3-inch floured cutter (push straight up and down; do not twist). Arrange on ungreased baking sheet, spacing ½ inch apart. Reroll scraps and cut out additional hearts. Brush tops with melted butter and sprinkle with sugar. Bake until just beginning to brown, about 12 minutes. Cool hearts for 5 minutes on rack before serving.

8 ❦ Crackers and Flatbreads

You may be so accustomed to thinking of breads in their usual loaf form that this chapter comes as something of a surprise. But in many parts of the world the most familiar breads are not loaves at all—consider, for example, Scandinavian hardtack, Armenian *lavash* and Indian *chapati*.

Those recipes are included here along with a selection of other crackers, wafers and flatbreads, both leavened and unleavened. They make particularly good cocktail fare; as an accompaniment to cheeses and dips they are far more interesting than purchased crackers. But the varied forms of these flatbreads make them intriguing any time. There are crisp wafers, chewy oatmeal Bannocks (page 107), golden deep-fried corn rounds (page 111) and attractively textured Scandinavian griddle breads made with a special knobbed rolling pin. The unleavened versions, in particular, are extremely quick and easy to prepare.

If you bake frequently these breads will be refreshingly out of the ordinary; if you are a novice at breadmaking you will be delighted by their simplicity. In any case, they are unusual and rewarding additions to any cook's repertoire.

Cinnamon Grahams

Makes about 5 dozen

1½ cups graham or whole wheat flour
1 cup all purpose flour
½ cup solid vegetable shortening, room temperature
⅓ cup firmly packed brown sugar
¼ cup honey
¼ cup vegetable oil

3 tablespoons cold water
1 teaspoon baking soda
1 teaspoon cinnamon
½ teaspoon salt

Additional all purpose flour

Mix all ingredients except additional flour in large bowl until smooth, using wooden spoon. Cover with plastic wrap and refrigerate 20 minutes.

Preheat oven to 425°F. Remove half of dough from refrigerator and place on ungreased baking sheet. Pat into smooth 4- to 5-inch square. Dust with additional all purpose flour and roll out on baking sheet to 10 × 12-inch rectangle. Cut dough into 2-inch squares, leaving in place on baking sheet. Prick entire surface with fork. Bake until golden, 7 to 10 minutes. Recut while hot if necessary. Cool on baking sheet. (Crackers crisp as they cool.) Repeat with remaining dough. Store crackers in airtight container.

Malted Crackers

String these crackers through a satin rope or a tasseled silk curtain cord and let guests help themselves. The crackers are best when freshly made.

Makes 12 to 15

1 teaspoon dry yeast
⅔ cup (about) warm water (105°F to 115°F)
2½ cups all purpose flour
2 tablespoons unflavored malt powder
1½ teaspoons baking powder
1 teaspoon salt

6 tablespoons (¾ stick) butter, chilled, cut into small pieces

Whipping cream
Coarse salt
Sesame seeds

Lightly oil baking sheet(s). Cut out 5-inch cardboard circle and set aside.

Dissolve yeast in warm water. Sift dry ingredients into large bowl. Using fingertips, quickly work in butter until no large flakes remain and butter is almost incorporated. Make well in center and add yeast, working dough with fingers until it forms compact mass slightly drier than firm pie pastry.

Turn dough out onto floured surface and divide in thirds. Work each portion through pasta machine with rollers at widest setting *(if dough feels at all damp, roll in flour each time it goes through machine to prevent sticking)*. Fold dough over and run through machine again for a total of 4 times.

Using cardboard pattern, cut circles from dough. Remove 1-inch circle from centers and set aside. Place large circles on baking sheet and make decorative pattern over surface using fork. Cover with plastic wrap and let stand in draft-free area 20 minutes. (Remaining dough can be reworked through machine to make additional circles.)

About 15 minutes before baking, preheat oven to 400°F. Brush circles lightly with cream. Sprinkle half of them with salt and the remaining half with sesame seeds. Bake 10 to 12 minutes. Cool crackers on racks. When cool, string onto satin rope or silk cord.

Wheat Germ Wafers

These crackers are good with cheese, vegetable dips and spreads.

Makes 32

1 cup whole wheat flour
½ cup wheat germ
¼ cup (½ stick) butter, room temperature
½ teaspoon salt
¼ cup (about) warm water

Additional wheat germ (optional)

Preheat oven to 450°F. Lightly grease baking sheets. Combine flour, wheat germ, butter and salt in large bowl. Rub against side of bowl with wooden spoon until butter is completely blended in. Stir in enough warm water to make crumbly dough. Turn out on lightly floured surface and knead briefly until dough is smooth. Divide into 8 balls. Cover with towel or plastic wrap to prevent drying.

Place 1 ball of dough on prepared baking sheet. Roll out into round 8 to 10 inches in diameter. Cut into 4 even wedges leaving in place on sheet. Brush with water and sprinkle with additional wheat germ if desired. Bake until wafers are dry and edges are crisp, about 5 minutes. Cut apart if necessary. Cool on rack. Repeat with remaining dough, cooling sheet between batches. (*While baking 1 wafer, roll another.*) Store in airtight container.

Scottish Currant Shortbread

This buttery, cookielike flatbread is good with afternoon tea or fruit soups.

Makes 2 dozen

⅓ cup dried currants
5 tablespoons fresh orange juice
1½ cups all purpose flour

2 tablespoons sugar
½ cup (1 stick) unsalted butter
Additional sugar

Preheat oven to 350°F. Lightly grease baking sheet. Bring currants and 4 tablespoons orange juice to boil in small saucepan. Stir; remove from heat and cool. Combine flour and sugar in large bowl. Cut in butter until mixture resembles coarse meal. Stir in currant mixture and remaining 1 tablespoon orange juice. Knead just until dough holds together. Roll dough out on prepared sheet into 10 × 12-inch rectangle. Trim edges and use scraps to square off corners. Prick entire surface with fork. Sprinkle with sugar. Cut into 24 squares, leaving in place on baking sheet. Bake until pale golden, 20 to 22 minutes. Recut while warm. Cool on rack. Store in airtight container.

Scottish Bannocks

A cross between a chewy oatmeal cookie and a biscuit. Serve fresh from the oven, as is or split and toasted. Excellent for breakfast or tea. Bannocks are best the day they are baked.

Makes 10 to 12

1½ cups all purpose flour
1 cup quick-cooking rolled oats
¼ cup (½ stick) butter, room temperature

2 tablespoons sugar
1 tablespoon baking powder
Pinch of salt
½ cup (about) milk

Preheat oven to 450°F. Combine flour, oats, butter, sugar, baking powder and salt in large bowl. Rub mixture against side of bowl with wooden spoon until butter is completely blended in. Slowly stir in enough milk to make stiff dough. Turn out onto lightly floured surface and knead just until dough holds together. Reflour surface lightly. Roll dough out ⅓ inch thick. Cut into 2½-inch rounds. Gather scraps together. Reroll and cut additional bannocks. Arrange on ungreased baking sheet, spacing 1 inch apart. Bake until light brown, 12 to 15 minutes. Serve hot or let cool on racks.

Oatmeal Hardtack

*This is a Scandinavian fa-
vorite. A square-cut
knobbed rolling pin (available in cookware stores) is
traditionally used to get a
pebbly texture, but a fork
can be substituted. Serve
hardtack with cheese or
soup.*

Makes about 5 dozen

¼ cup solid vegetable shortening,
   room temperature
¼ cup sugar
 2 tablespoons (¼ stick) butter,
   room temperature
1¾ cups all purpose flour
 1 cup regular or quick-cooking
   rolled oats

½ teaspoon salt
½ teaspoon baking soda
¾ cup buttermilk

   Additional rolled oats

Cream shortening, sugar and butter in large bowl until smooth. Combine flour,
oats, salt and soda in small bowl. Add dry ingredients to creamed mixture alternately with buttermilk, blending to form stiff dough. Cover and refrigerate
for 30 minutes.

   Preheat oven to 325°F. Grease two 14 × 17-inch baking sheets. Sprinkle with
oats. Remove half of dough from refrigerator. Shape into smooth square on
generously floured board. Transfer to prepared baking sheet. Pat and press dough
to flatten as much as possible, then roll out to edges of pan with rolling pin; trim
edges. To give pebbly texture, roll over entire surface with hardtack rolling pin,
or prick surface evenly with fork. Cut into 2 × 3-inch pieces using pastry wheel
or knife, leaving in place on baking sheet. Bake until crisp and golden, 15 to 20
minutes. Recut crackers if necessary. Cool on racks. Repeat with remaining dough.
Store in airtight container.

Armenian Flatbread (Lavash)

*To serve with dips or
spreads, break up and use
crisp. For sandwiches,
moisten both sides of
bread, shaking off excess
water. Place between
pieces of plastic wrap and
let stand 20 minutes (or
wrap in damp towel for 30
minutes).*

Makes 8

2 cups warm water (105°F to
   115°F)
1 tablespoon sugar
1 envelope dry yeast
4½ to 5 cups bread flour or all
   purpose flour

½ cup (1 stick) butter, melted and
   cooled
1 tablespoon salt

Combine water and sugar in large bowl. Stir in yeast. Let mixture stand until
bubbly, 5 to 10 minutes. Beat in 2 cups flour, butter and salt until smooth. Slowly
add enough of remaining flour to make stiff dough. Turn out onto lightly floured
surface; invert bowl over top. Let rest 15 minutes.

   Knead dough on lightly floured surface until smooth and satiny, adding more
flour as necessary to prevent sticking, about 10 minutes (dough should remain
soft and light). Grease large bowl. Add dough, turning to coat entire surface.
Cover with plastic wrap. Let rise in warm draft-free area until doubled, about 1
to 1½ hours.

   Preheat oven to 375°F. Grease baking sheet or pizza pan. Punch dough down
and divide into 8 pieces. Cover with plastic wrap. Knead 1 piece for 2 minutes
and form into ball. Place on lightly floured surface and roll out into 12-inch
circle. Roll up on rolling pin and unroll onto prepared pan. Bake until dough
bubbles, bottom begins to brown slightly and bread is crisp, 10 to 12 minutes.
Immediately remove from baking sheet and cool on rack. Repeat with remaining
dough. *(While baking 1 bread, roll another.)* Store in airtight container.

Graham Flatbrød Cigars

After baking, the flat-breads are rolled up into cigar shapes. Serve whole or slice diagonally. Great for breakfast or with soups or mixed green salads.

Makes 8 cigar-shaped breads or about 48 2-inch crackers

1½ **cups graham or whole wheat flour**
1 **cup all purpose flour**
1 **tablespoon butter, melted**
1 **teaspoon sugar**
1 **teaspoon salt**

1½ **cups (about) boiling water**

Additional all purpose flour
¼ **cup (½ stick) butter, melted**

Combine graham flour, all purpose flour, 1 tablespoon butter, sugar and salt in large bowl. Stir in enough boiling water to make stiff dough. Cover dough and let stand until cool, about 1 hour.

Lightly flour work surface. Divide dough into 8 balls. Roll each out into round about 12 inches in diameter, flouring surface as necessary. Lightly sprinkle with flour, stack and cover. Heat electric griddle to 450°F (or heat griddle or heavy skillet over high heat until drop of water bounces off surface). Add 1 round and cook, turning once, until leathery, 30 seconds to 1 minute on each side. Remove from griddle. Immediately brush with melted butter and roll up tightly into cigar shape. Repeat with remaining pieces of dough. Leave whole or cut diagonally into 2-inch-long pieces. Serve warm or at room temperature.

Can be frozen up to 1 month.

Sultsina

This rye flatbread from eastern Finland is filled with a cooked farina mix-ture. It is traditionally served as a snack with hot coffee or tea.

Makes 4

Filling
½ **cup milk**
¼ **teaspoon salt**
2 **tablespoons farina**
1 **tablespoon butter, room temperature**
3 **to 4 tablespoons whipping cream**

Rye Dough
½ **cup warm water**

1 **tablespoon butter, melted**
¼ **teaspoon salt**
½ **cup all purpose flour**
½ **cup rye flour**
Additional all purpose flour

Melted butter
Cinnamon sugar

For filling: Bring milk to boil in small saucepan over medium heat. Add salt, then slowly stir in farina until smooth. Return to boil and cook 1 minute, stirring constantly. Remove from heat. Cover and let stand 3 minutes. Stir in butter and enough cream to make mixture spreadable. Cover filling to keep warm while preparing dough.

For dough: Combine water, butter and salt in medium bowl. Beat in all purpose flour until smooth, using wooden spoon. Mix in rye flour. Turn dough out onto floured surface and knead until smooth, about 2 minutes, adding more all purpose flour if dough is sticky. Shape into cylinder; cut into 4 pieces. Dust with flour. Reflour surface lightly. Pat each piece into small round cake. Roll into 8-inch rounds. Flour tops of rounds lightly. Stack; cover with plastic wrap.

Heat electric griddle to 450°F (or heat griddle or heavy skillet over high heat until drop of water bounces off surface). Cook 1 dough round, turning once, until dry and spotted with brown but still pliable, about 30 seconds on each side. Transfer to warm platter. Repeat with remaining dough.

Spread 2 tablespoons filling down center of each sultsina. Fold 2 opposite edges over filling, just meeting in center, then fold in half again lengthwise. Cut into 2-inch pieces, if desired. Serve immediately with butter and cinnamon sugar for dipping.

This recipe can be doubled.

Norwegian Potato Lefse

Delicious spread with butter and eaten warm, Lefse is the bread that turns a Norwegian meal into a celebration. In Norway the breads are rolled out with a grooved (lefse) rolling pin, but a standard pin also works well.

Makes 8

1¾ pounds russet potatoes
1 cup all purpose flour
2 tablespoons (¼ stick) unsalted butter or lard, melted

1 teaspoon salt
¼ cup warm milk

Bring potatoes to boil with water to cover in medium saucepan. Cook until easily pierced in center with knife. Drain. Peel potatoes; cool *completely*. Put potatoes through ricer or shred coarsely. Transfer 2 cups potatoes to bowl. Blend in flour, butter and salt. Stir in milk to form smooth dough. Cover and let stand 15 minutes.

Divide dough into 8 balls; cover. Heat electric griddle to 450°F (or heat griddle or heavy skillet over high heat until drop of water bounces off surface). Flour work surface lightly. Roll 1 ball out into very thin circle (almost transparent), about 10 inches in diameter. Cook until covered with tiny brown flecks, about 1 minute on each side. Remove from griddle and fold into quarters. Repeat rolling and cooking with remaining balls, stacking folded breads. If not serving immediately, wrap with plastic to prevent drying.

Can be frozen up to 6 weeks. Reheat in 300°F oven 10 to 15 minutes.

Swedish Rye Tack

The surface of this chewy, fennel-flavored bread is classically textured with a square-cut knobbed rolling pin. Use rye tack for sandwiches.

Makes two 13-inch rounds

¼ cup warm water (105°F to 115°F)
1 envelope dry yeast
4 tablespoons light molasses or dark corn syrup
1 cup milk, scalded and cooled to 105°F to 115°F
½ cup (1 stick) unsalted butter, melted and cooled

1½ teaspoons fennel seeds, crushed
¾ teaspoon salt
3 cups rye flour
1¼ cups (about) bread flour or all purpose flour

Pour water into large bowl. Stir in yeast and 1 tablespoon molasses. Let stand until bubbly, about 5 minutes. Add remaining molasses, milk, butter, fennel and salt. Mix in rye flour with wooden spoon until smooth. Stir in enough bread flour to make stiff dough. Turn out onto floured surface. Cover dough and let rest for 1 hour.

Grease 2 baking sheets. Knead dough until smooth and satiny, about 10 minutes. Divide dough into 2 pieces. Form 1 into ball. Roll out directly on 1 prepared sheet into 13-inch round, preferably using hardtack or knobbed rolling pin. (If not available, roll out with rolling pin, then prick entire surface with fork.) Cut out 2-inch hole in center of round, using beverage glass or cookie cutter. Repeat with remaining dough. Cover and let rise in warm area until puffy, about 45 minutes.

Preheat oven to 425°F. Bake breads until brown around edges and firm, 15 to 20 minutes. Transfer to kitchen towels. Brush with warm water and cover with towels. Cool. Store in airtight container. Cut in wedges to serve.

Pakistani Nan

These chewy little bread rounds are a fine accompaniment to a meal, or use as "scoops" for hummus and other dips.

Makes 12

1 envelope dry yeast
1 cup warm water (105°F to 115°F)

1 teaspoon salt
2¼ cups all purpose or bread flour

Grease large bowl and set aside. Dissolve yeast in water in another large bowl. Add salt and slowly stir in flour to form stiff dough. Turn out onto lightly floured surface and knead until smooth and elastic, about 10 minutes. Place in greased bowl, turning to coat. Cover and let rise in warm draft-free area until doubled, about 1 hour.

Grease 3 baking sheets. Punch dough down and turn out onto lightly oiled surface. Knead briefly. Divide dough into 12 balls. Roll each ball out into 4- to 5-inch round. Place 4 rounds on each sheet. Let rise in warm draft-free area until almost doubled, 30 minutes.

Preheat oven to 500°F. Bake breads until just puffed and edges appear brown, 5 to 7 minutes. Serve warm or at room temperature.

Can be wrapped tightly and frozen up to 1 month.

Chippewa Indian Fried Bread

Traditionally this bread is slapped with the fingertips into flat rounds. It is delicious with coffee or tea.

Makes 8

2½ cups all purpose flour
1½ tablespoons baking powder
1 teaspoon salt
¾ cup warm water
1 tablespoon vegetable oil

1 tablespoon nonfat dry milk powder

Vegetable oil (for deep frying)
Cinnamon sugar

Combine flour, baking powder and salt in large bowl. Combine water, oil and dry milk powder and stir into flour mixture until smooth dough forms. Turn out onto lightly floured surface. Knead 4 times into smooth ball. Cover and let rest 10 minutes.

Divide dough into 8 balls. Flatten with fingertips or roll out each ball to form 8- to 10-inch round. Make small hole in center of each with finger or handle of wooden spoon. Lightly flour rounds, stack and cover with towel or plastic wrap. Heat about 1 inch oil to 375°F in large skillet. Gently place 1 bread round in hot fat and cook until golden and crisp, 1 to 2 minutes on each side. Drain on paper towels. Repeat with remaining dough. Serve bread hot or at room temperature, sprinkled with cinnamon sugar.

Hot Water Corn Bread

4 to 5 servings

2 cups water
½ cup chopped green onion
1 teaspoon salt
1 teaspoon sugar
1 teaspoon freshly ground pepper

1 cup yellow cornmeal
1 cup white cornmeal

Vegetable oil (for deep frying)

Bring 2 cups water to boil with onion, salt, sugar and pepper. Turn off heat. Combine cornmeals and add ⅓ to water in thin stream, stirring constantly until very thick. Vigorously stir in remainder. Cool to room temperature.

Form cornmeal mixture into 3-inch rounds ½ inch thick. Heat oil in deep fryer or large saucepan to 350°F. Fry rounds in batches (do not crowd) until golden brown, about 1 minute per side. Transfer to paper towels using slotted spoon. Serve immediately.

Indian Chapati

A classic bread to serve with curries. Poori, another Indian bread made from the same dough, is cooked in deep fat instead of on a dry griddle.

Makes 8

2 cups whole wheat flour
¹/₂ cup all purpose flour
1 teaspoon salt
¹/₂ cup (1 stick) butter, melted
6 tablespoons warm water

Additional melted butter

Combine whole wheat flour, all purpose flour and salt in large bowl. Stir in butter and warm water to make smooth dough. Turn out onto lightly floured surface and knead 3 to 4 times, until smooth ball forms. Cover dough with towel and let rest for 1 hour.

Divide dough into 8 balls. Roll each out into 8-inch round. Dust with flour, stack and cover with towel or plastic wrap. Heat electric griddle to 450°F (or heat griddle or skillet over high heat until drop of water bounces off surface).* Cook chapatis, one at a time, until flecked with brown spots, about 2 minutes on each side. Brush with melted butter and stack as removed from griddle. Wrap to keep warm and pliable. Serve immediately.

Chapati can be frozen up to 1 month.

*For poori, heat 1 inch vegetable oil in large skillet to 375°F. Fry dough rounds one at a time until puffed, bubbly and brown, about 2 minutes per side. Serve immediately.

Rieska

This unleavened bread of Finland must be served right from the oven, spread with butter. Great with morning coffee or hot soup.

Makes one 12-inch flatbread

¹/₂ cup buttermilk
¹/₂ cup whipping cream
1 tablespoon butter, melted
¹/₂ teaspoon salt

¹/₂ teaspoon sugar
1 cup barley flour* or ¹/₂ cup *each* rye flour and whole wheat flour

Preheat oven to 450°F. Butter 12-inch pizza pan. Mix buttermilk, cream, butter, salt and sugar in large bowl. Stir in flour to make smooth dough. Spread dough evenly in pan. Bake until lightly browned around edges, about 15 minutes. Cut into wedges and serve.

*Available at natural food stores.

Savory Cheese Wafers

Easy crackers with a zesty flavor.

Makes about 10 dozen

1 pound cheddar cheese, grated
3 cups all purpose flour
1 cup (2 sticks) butter, room temperature

1 teaspoon salt
¹/₄ teaspoon ground red pepper
1 cup chopped pecans

Beat first 5 ingredients with electric mixer until well combined. Mix in pecans. Divide dough into thirds. Form each into smooth 1¹/₂-inch diameter log on sheet of waxed paper. Wrap tightly. Refrigerate at least 1 hour to firm. *(Can be prepared ahead and refrigerated 3 days, or frozen several months. Thaw in refrigerator before continuing.)*

Preheat oven to 325°F. Remove paper from dough. Cut dough into ¹/₄-inch-thick slices. Arrange 1¹/₂ inches apart on baking sheets. Bake until golden brown, 15 to 18 minutes. Transfer to paper towels and cool completely. Store airtight.

Herbed French Bread Chips

A lovely accompaniment to soups. The bread recipe yields three loaves: Use one for the chips and save the other two for later in the week.

Makes 4 cups chips

1 envelope dry yeast
1 teaspoon sugar
¼ cup warm water (105°F to 115°F)

1 cup water, room temperature
2 tablespoons (¼ stick) butter, melted
2½ to 3 cups unbleached all purpose flour
3 tablespoons nonfat dry milk powder
1¼ to 1½ teaspoons salt

2 tablespoons minced fresh thyme or 1 teaspoon dried, crumbled
2 tablespoons minced fresh sage or 1 teaspoon dried, crumbled
1 tablespoon minced fresh Italian parsley
1 tablespoon minced fresh oregano or ½ teaspoon dried, crumbled
2 tablespoons (¼ stick) butter, melted

Sprinkle yeast and sugar over ¼ cup warm water in large bowl; stir to dissolve. Let stand until foamy.

Butter large bowl. Blend 1 cup water and 1 tablespoon melted butter into yeast mixture. Combine 2½ cups flour, milk powder and salt. Stir into yeast mixture ½ cup at a time to form slightly sticky dough, adding up to ½ cup more flour if necessary. Turn dough out onto lightly floured surface and knead until smooth and elastic, about 5 minutes. Add dough to prepared bowl, turning to coat entire surface. Cover and let rise in warm draft-free area until dough is doubled in volume, about 1¼ hours.

Generously butter triple French bread pan or baking sheet. Combine herbs. Punch dough down. Turn out onto lightly floured surface and knead in herbs. Cut dough into 3 pieces. Roll each out into 8 × 15-inch rectangle. Starting with long side, roll dough up into cylinder. Tuck ends under and pinch seam to seal. Place seam side down in prepared pan. Cover with waxed paper and towel. Let dough rise until doubled in volume, about 1 hour.

Preheat oven to 375°F. Brush loaves with 1 tablespoon melted butter. Bake until golden and loaves sound hollow when tapped on bottom, about 20 minutes. Cool completely on rack. Wrap 2 loaves and store for later use. Let remaining loaf stand at room temperature, unwrapped, overnight.

Preheat oven to 300°F. Cut unwrapped loaf into ¹⁄₁₆- to ⅛-inch-thick slices. Arrange slices in single layer on baking sheet. Brush lightly with remaining melted butter. Bake until slices are dry and beginning to brown around edges, about 10 minutes. Transfer to another baking sheet. Cool completely before serving. (*Can be prepared 1 week ahead and stored at room temperature in plastic bags.*)

Hallie's Corn Crackers

Makes about 8 dozen

2 cups sifted all purpose flour
2 teaspoons baking powder
½ teaspoon salt
½ cup (1 stick) unsalted butter, room temperature
2 tablespoons sugar

2 eggs, room temperature
1 cup milk
1 cup water
½ cup white cornmeal
Fennel seeds or cumin seeds

Preheat oven to 375°F. Sift flour, baking powder and salt. Cream butter with electric mixer until fluffy. Mix in sugar. Beat in eggs one at a time. Combine milk and water and blend into batter alternately with flour mixture in 3 additions each, using low speed. Mix in cornmeal. Strain batter.

Heat 10½ × 15½-inch jelly roll pan in oven 1 minute. Butter pan. Pour in ⅔ cup batter, tilting to coat bottom evenly. Sprinkle with ½ teaspoon fennel or cumin seeds. Bake until edges brown and batter is firm enough to cut, about 5 minutes. Cut into 16 rectangular crackers. Continue baking until golden brown and crisp, about 15 minutes. Transfer to paper towels. Repeat with remaining batter. Wash and dry pan between batches. Cool crackers completely before serving. (*Can be stored in airtight container up to 1 week.*)

For variation, stir ½ teaspoon ground red pepper into ⅔ cup batter.

🍐 Index

Credits and Acknowledgments

The following people contributed the recipes included in this book:

Alderbrook, Brush Prairie, Washington
Linda Anderson
Sandi Anderson
Patricia Baird
Joan Baxley
The Bostonian, Boston, Massachusetts
Giuliano Bugialli
The Buttery, Santa Monica, California
Sharon Cadwallader
Anna Teresa Callen
Marina Castle
The Catnip Mouse,
    Riverton, Connecticut
Molly Chappellet
Nodie Clancy
Mary Beth Clark
Elyn Clarkson
Maggi Dahlgren
Diane Darrow
Narsai David
Deirdre Davis
The Dobbin House,
    Gettysburg, Pennsylvania
The Dog Team Tavern,
    Middlebury, Vermont
Celesta Drobny
Elizabeth on 37th, Savannah, Georgia
Naomi French
The Gosby House Inn,
    Pacific Grove, California
Janet Grady
Bob and Beverly Green
Freddi Greenberg
Greenwood Lodge, Elk, California
Maureen V. Gribben
Beth Hensperger
Sam Higgins
Jeanne Howard
Susan F. Jarek-Glidden
Jean's Soup & Sandwich Place,
    Milwaukie, Oregon
Jane Helsel Joseph

Lynne Kasper
Ouida and Vince Kelly
Kelly's French Pastry Shop,
    Santa Cruz, California
Kristine Kidd
Jean Kressy
La Mexicana Bakery,
    San Francisco, California
Honey Lesser
Jeanne Lundgren
Dianne Lynch
Abby Mandel
Tom Maresca
Linda Marino
Marriott's Casa Marina Resort,
    Key West, Florida
Richard McCullough
Sara McNulty
The Milk Pail, Dundee, Illinois
Henry Miller
Aline Mobley
Jinx and Jefferson Morgan
Della Nevans
Lila and Norm Nielsen
Beatrice Ojakangas
Judith Olney
Fenella Pearson
Cynthia A. Pierce
Laurie Polansky
Thelma Pressman
Tim Pyatt
Raffles Bar & Grill, Miami, Florida
Carolyn Reagan
Ruedell Reaves
Sandy Ringel
Joan Robinson
Betty Rosbottom
Sandy Beach, Barbados, West Indies
Norma Schechner
Gillian Servais
Edena Sheldon
Shirley Slater

Rita M. Sorci
Douglas Spingler
Lucille Stakee
Connie Stapleton
Bonnie Stern
Terwilliger's Tavern, Montgomery, Ohio
Tolly's, Oakland, Oregon
Mark Trevor
Tu Tu'Tun Lodge, Gold Beach, Oregon
Wine Country Inn, St. Helena,
    California
Yankee Clipper Inn,
    Rockport, Massachusetts

Additional text was supplied by:
Faye Levy, *About Yeast; Baking Soda
    and Baking Powder*
Jan Weimer, *About Flours*

The Knapp Press
is a wholly owned subsidiary of
KNAPP COMMUNICATIONS CORPORATION.
Chairman and Chief Executive Officer:
    Cleon T. Knapp
President: H. Stephen Cranston
Senior Vice-Presidents:
    Betsy Wood Knapp
        (*MIS Electronic Media*)
    Harry Myers
        (*Magazine Group Publisher*)
    William J. N. Porter
        (*Corporate Product Sales*)
    Paige Rense (*Editorial*)

Editor, Bon Appétit: Marilou Vaughan
Art Director, Bon Appétit:
    Bernard Rotondo
Associate Editor, The Knapp Press:
    Patricia Connell
Rights and Permissions Coordinator:
    Karen Legier
Indexer: Rose Grant

Composition by Publisher's Typography

This book is set in Sabon, a face designed by Jan Teischold in 1967 and based on early fonts
engraved by Garamond and Granjon.